Rediscovering Christianity

Rediscovering Christianity
First Edition (2024)
Copyright (c) A Call to Repentance

ISBN 978-1-7636774-0-1

This work is licensed under Creative Commons Attribution-NonCommercial-NoDerivatives 4.0 International. To view a copy of this license, visit https://creativecommons.org/licenses/by-nc-nd/4.0/. All rights not explicitly granted by this license are reserved.

All correspondence with regard to this copyright notice or any other aspect of this book should be directed to: contact@calltorepentance.org

Editor's Foreword

Johann Arndt's "True Christianity," was first published in 1605 and quickly became the most frequently printed and widely read book in Protestantism after the Bible. In its day it was translated into thirty languages[1,2,3]. It heavily influenced both the Lutheran and the reformed churches across Europe and England in the form of Pietism and Puritanism, and came to define the faith and spirit of a large part of Protestantism. The well-known Puritan minister John Flavel quoted extensively from it in his "The Method of Grace in the Gospel Revealed." A century later, John Wesley relied on Arndt's thoughts in the development of Methodism. While now largely lost, the true spirit of Protestantism cannot be comprehended without embracing Arndt's work, and this is the motivation for presenting this work anew today.

This book consists of two parts: Book I is an abridged and restructured adaptation of Johann Arndt's "True Christianity" in modern English, and Book II contains additional explanations of the main themes discussed in Book I along with other supporting material. The second book examines the common understanding of the foundations of Christianity in the light of the teachings of Jesus. There are many forms of godliness, but only one true godliness. There are many Christs but only one true Lord of heaven and earth. This book aims to answer the question of what is that Christianity that Jesus will recognise as His Own when He returns to sort out the sheep from the goats. What does having faith actually mean? What is the repentance that will not need to be repented of? What does being born again mean in practice? How does true godliness differ from a form of godliness? What does it mean to be holy in this life? What does it mean to fear of God? All these questions and more strike at the heart of popular Christianity. The answers to these questions will determine whether true Christianity is just another comforting, self-serving religion, or a fundamentally unique movement with the power to vitally transform man in the context of a dying world.

---

[1] Prof. J. S. O'Malley, "Recovering "true Christianity" in *Christian History* Magazine, No.151 (2024)

[2] Rev. Dr. Joseph Augustus Seiss, quoted in Charles F. Schaeffer's introduction to his revision of "True Christianity" (1868) Philadelphia

[3] First extant translation into English was made by Radulphus Castrensis Antimachivalensis and printed in London by Mat. Simmons for H. Blunden at the Castle in Corn-hill, (1646).

Contents

Book I: True Christianity

- Introduction 1
- Chapter 1: The Image of God in Man 5
- Chapter 2: The Fall of Man. 10
- Chapter 3. How Man Is Restored In Christ 15
- Chapter 4. Repentance the Key to Redemption 22
- Chapter 5: Righteousness by Faith 29
- Chapter 6. Living by Every Word of God 35
- Chapter 7. Blessed are they that Mourn 39
- Chapter 8. Love God with All Your Heart 44
- Chapter 9. Pilgrims and Strangers 50
- Chapter 10. Christian Warfare 56

Book II: Understanding Christianity

- Introduction 65
- Saving Faith 69
- True Repentance 74
- The New Birth 79
- The Kingdom of God 84
- Are You Saved? 89
- The Grace of God 94
- True Godliness 100
- Holiness 105
- God's Law 110
- Forgiveness 115
- Godly Fear 120
- False Christs 125

Book I: True Christianity

An abridgement of Johann Arndt's "True Christianity" (1605).

2Pet 3:9 The Lord is not slack concerning his promise, as some men count slackness; but is longsuffering to us-ward, not willing that any should perish, but that all should come to repentance.

Matt 7:21 - 23 Not everyone that saith unto me, Lord, Lord, shall enter into the kingdom of heaven; but he that doeth the will of my Father which is in heaven. Many will say to me in that day, Lord, Lord, have we not prophesied in thy name? and in thy name have cast out devils? and in thy name done many wonderful works? And then will I profess unto them, I never knew you: depart from me, ye that work iniquity.

Introduction

Dear Christian reader, it is distressing to see the gospel of Christ misunderstood and misused in our time. Many claim to be followers of Christ, but deny Him by their behaviour. Stripped of its external rituals and specific dogma, their religion is not very different from that of the heathen. True Christianity is not just about believing in Christ, but about living in accordance with His teachings and example. It is about having a living and active faith that receives from Christ all that is good, righteous, and blessed and reveals itself in genuine godliness and the fruits of repentance. While faith is itself invisible, its fruit must be seen in words and actions. A faith that is barren of the fruit of righteousness is dead. It is not enough to know the word of God; we must obey it in practice.

Many people view theology as a mere intellectual pursuit, but it should be a living experience, a practical exercise. Everyone today strives for greatness and recognition, but few make an effort to cultivate true piety. They are content with a superficial knowledge, but no one can truly love Christ, who does not seek "to know the love of Christ" and "be filled with all the fullness of God." (Eph. 3:19). While many eagerly seek out experts in different fields to gain knowledge and skill; few are willing to learn from the greatest Teacher of all, Jesus Christ, how to become meek and humble. Yet His holy life is the only sure guide for our life and conduct, and opens to us true wisdom and knowledge.

True Christianity does not consist in words or external display, but in a life that is inwardly transformed by living faith in Christ. This transformation of our innermost being is the fruit of a deep and abiding repentance, without which, faith degenerates into presumption. Here is where many Christians make a mistake; they are not renewed by the word of God in practice, and do not become new creatures. We must become new creations of the Holy Spirit by putting off our old sinful nature. This involves a change of the heart, mind, and affections in conformance to Christ. Those who call themselves Christians should do so because they actually live in Christ and He lives in them. In a word, Adam must die, and Christ must live in us.

Do not confuse the righteousness that is by faith, without which no one can be saved, and the righteousness of a Christian life. Without the first, which is the inward transformation of the soul, the second, its outworking in the life, cannot appear. Outward Christianity may be the fruit of that transformation or it may just be a religious veneer. Do not associate your religious sentiments, good deeds, morals, virtues, or various gifts with your acceptance before God. While these may be admirable, they do not necessarily proceed from true faith, nor do they count towards salvation, which is based solely on the righteousness of Jesus Christ, grasped through repentance and faith. Since the evidence of something cannot be its cause, the only evidence of that transformation, can also not be faith but can only be an abiding inward repentance, one that only you and God can see. If, instead, you are grateful to God because you feel that He has in some way made you more righteous than others, so that you no longer need to repent as they do, then you do not understand the righteousness of God.

All true Christian virtues – true hope, sincere love, persevering patience, earnest prayer, Christian humility, and a childlike fear of God – are born, and they cannot be obtained from Christ without abiding repentance and faith. Repentance is the fountain of meekness, humility, contrition, surrender, diffidence and dependence on God. Hope is born when in contrition, faith embraces the blessings promised by God. Love is born when in humility, faith shares with others the blessings it has received from God. Patience is born when in meekness faith endures trials in submission to God's will. Prayer is born when, in dependence on God, faith groans under the burden of the cross or praises God for His mercies. And when in the absence of self-assurance this faith earnestly strives to keep the grace of God, or, as Paul says: "work out your own salvation with fear and trembling" (Phil. 2:12), then the fear of God is born. Without abiding repentance, no hope, love, patience, prayer, or Christian humility can be acceptable to God. Just as faith without repentance is presumption, hope without contrition is self-indulgence, charity without humility is self-serving, patience without meekness is obstinacy. Prayer without dependence is, at best, small-talk, at worst, imposition, and fear without humility becomes defiance.

It is one thing to serve or obey Christ but quite another to follow Him. He says: "If any man serve me, let him follow me." (John 12:26). Many, like the rich young ruler, are happy to do the former, but will not closely follow His example. He who truly loves Christ will love the example of His holy life, His

Introduction

humility, meekness, patience, and willingness to suffer inconvenience, shame, and contempt, and will accompany Him, even if doing so is painful. We should strive to imitate Christ's holy life more fully, for this is the only way we can live in Christ, and have Christ live in us, as John: says "He that saith he abideth in him ought himself also so to walk, even as he walked." (1 John 2:6).

Many are ashamed of Christ's holy example, His humility and lowly condition, they desire a Christ of pleasing appearance, who is polished, affluent, self-confident and in line with the values, priorities, and trends of the world. No one desires to follow Christ as He truly is: poor, meek, despised, and lowly. Christ says, "Whosoever shall be ashamed of me and of my words... of him also shall the Son of man be ashamed," (Mark 8:38), Will you hear Him say on judgment day: "I never knew you." You were not willing to know me in my humility, and therefore I do not know you in your pride?

Not only does ungodliness, even among professed Christians, contradict Christ and true Christianity, but also leads to the accumulation of God's displeasure and His wrath. As a result, all of creation is increasingly against us, and we can expect to face afflictions: war, famine, and pestilence. The hour of His judgement is near. A time of tribulation is coming. The terrible plagues that afflicted the Egyptians before the exodus of Israel are a foreshadowing of the dreadful plagues that will come upon the ungodly and the unrepentant before God's redemption. The Scriptures are filled with warnings of God's jealousy and calls for true repentance, without which eternal salvation cannot be obtained. It is therefore high time to repent, to turn from the world, to truly believe in Him, and be transformed in thought and conduct, so that we may securely "dwell in the secret place of the Most High, and abide under the shadow of the Almighty." (Ps. 91:1). Jesus says: "Watch ye therefore, and pray always, that ye may be accounted worthy to escape all these things." (Luke 21:36).

Do not imagine that repentance is a light or easy task. It is not a matter of merely going through the motions, but of genuinely surrendering our lives to God. It is a task that requires great humility and a willingness to cut away from ourselves, and anchor our souls to Christ. The Apostle Paul, in solemn words, commands us to mortify and crucify the old man of the flesh with its affections and desires; to offer our bodies as a living sacrifice; to die unto sin;

and to be crucified unto the world. (Col. 3:5; Rom. 6:6; 12:1; 1 Pet. 2:24; Gal. 5:24; 6:14). This cannot be achieved while we gratify our pride and selfishness.

Nor do the holy prophets casually suggest that we have a humble and contrite heart, instead saying "Rend your heart" and "weep and lament" (Joel 2:13, 17; Jer 4:8). Alluding to it, the Lord Jesus Christ demanded that we deny ourselves and renounce all that we have, even ourselves, if we want to follow Him (Luk 9:23; Mat 16:24). It is only with such repentance that the consolation of the gospel is obtained. But where is such repentance now to be found? This kind of repentance cannot come from a superficial, frivolous or careless mind set, but rather from a deeply humbled heart, and it is solely through the Spirit of God, working through the Word, that we can experience genuine repentance.

Repentance must be your urgent concern. Without it, you cannot have a genuine faith that can transform your heart. You cannot truly experience the consolation of the gospel; joy, peace and hope, unless you have first experienced a heartfelt and sincere godly sorrow for sin that results in a broken spirit and contrite heart. As it is written, "to the poor the gospel is preached" (Luke 7:22), and "blessed are the poor in spirit" (Mat 5:3) implying that true repentance is necessary for the Gospel to be effective. Faith can only bring life to the heart if it has first been put to death by sorrow that is rooted in a deep realisation of our sinfulness. Without this kind of sorrow, faith is incomplete and ineffective.

The goal of this book is to describe what such a sincere and earnest repentance of the heart is like, and how true faith is revealed in the life and behaviour. To do so it must clearly explain the misery and helplessness of man; teach us to put no trust in ourselves or our ability; take away everything from ourselves; and to ascribe all to Christ, so that He alone may dwell in us, work all things in us, and create all things in us, because He is the beginning, middle, and end, of our conversion and salvation. This is the true doctrine of justification and righteousness by faith.

Chapter 1: The Image of God in Man

Be renewed in the spirit of your mind; and... put on the new man, which after God is created in righteousness and true holiness. – Eph. 4:23, 24.

God is a spirit (Joh 4:24): infinite in understanding, holiness and power, whereas man is "but flesh" (Ps 78:39): finite and fail. The term "flesh" encompasses not just physical aspects of man's body: his bones, muscles, tendons, nerves, and brain, but also its functions and capacities, both physical and mental including man's thoughts, feelings, emotions, and desires: his psyche (Mat 26:41; Rom 8:7,5; 7:5; Gal 5:19-20). Man was, however, to be more than just another animal upon the earth, as the apostle Paul writes, "all flesh is not the same flesh: but there is one kind of flesh of men, another flesh of beasts..." (1 Cor 15:39). God's intention in making mankind was to "dwell in them, and walk in them" (2Cor 6:16). Accordingly, the Bible likens man to a vessel of clay created by the divine potter (Isa 64:8; Lam 4:2). Just as potters craft beautiful vessels for keeping and conveying substances and displaying their creativity and skill, so too, man's 'flesh' was set apart from all other creatures (Job 7:17; Ps 8:4-6) and made to contain and reveal the majesty, splendour, and beauty of God's character as well as His power, wisdom, and goodness.

Into this flesh, God breathed "the breath of life" (Gen 2:7). By this God did not just give man life like He did to all other creatures that breathe "wherein there is life" (Gen 1:30) but He also put in man His Holy Spirit. The same word translated as 'breath' (in Gen 2:7) is translated as 'spirit' in "the spirit of man is the candle of the LORD" (Prov 20:27). As Jesus declared "the words that I speak unto you, they are spirit, and they are life" (Joh 6:63) so the Psalmist can say "Thy word is a lamp unto my feet, and a light unto my path" (Ps 119:105). In putting His Holy Spirit in man, God made Adam into a shining light, reflecting and revealing His glory and the words of scripture were fulfilled: "Arise, shine; for thy light is come, and the glory of the LORD is risen upon thee" (Isa 60:1). The spirit of God in man was God's divine imprint, mark, monogram, or seal (Eph 1:13); the finishing touch of his workmanship. The spirit in man (Job 32:8) is his highest governing authority, influencing his character, which in turn shapes his thoughts, emotions, will, understanding and desires. These control man's words and actions, effectively determining every aspect of his behaviour and shaping the trajectory of his life. In making man's flesh a vessel for His own spirit, God intended it to be the controlling influence and ultimate source of motivation, direction and inspiration for every facet of his life. As a lamp of clay holds the oil that burns within it to produce light so the spirit of God was to animate the flesh of man to produce every good work (2Tim 2:21). He intended to do His work through man, "for it is God who works in you both to will and to do of his good pleasure." (Phil 2:13) and "thou also hast wrought all our works in us." (Isa 26:12) As the scripture says, "we have this treasure in earthen vessels, that the excellency of the power may be of God, and not of us (2 Cor 4:7).

By putting His spirit in man, God designed man to reflect His holiness, righteousness, and goodness. God's purpose was to illuminate man's understanding, guide his will, and shape his affections, and be revealed in his daily life and behaviour. As a result, all man's actions, both inward and outward, would reveal nothing but divine love, purity, and power, so that man's life on earth would resemble that of the angels in heaven, who are always engaged in doing the will of their Heavenly Father. This is what God meant when he said, "Let us make man in our image, after our likeness." (Gen 1:26).

God intended to delight and rejoice in man, just as a father rejoices when he beholds himself *or another self* in his own child. As God gazed upon man, reflecting His own perfect character, He was pleased and delighted. As described in Proverbs 8:31, "my delights were with the sons of men." It was God's greatest joy to behold man, the crowning masterpiece of His creation, and He rested as it were, in the knowledge that in man's perfect innocence and beauty, the glory of His own character would be fully revealed. Since everything in nature gravitates to its own kind, and finds pleasure in that which is similar, it follows that man having been created in the likeness of God, was thereby prepared to receive and relate to God. Additionally, God was also ready to share Himself with man, bestowing upon him all the treasures of His goodness and all its blessings. God intended man to always enjoy this wonderful relation with Him, had man continued to reflect His likeness and fulfil His purposes.

The essence of an image is that it accurately represents the object it intends to convey. An image reflected in a mirror is never as radiant as the original, and the clarity of the reflection depends to the quality of the mirror itself. Similarly, the image of God becomes more or less visible depending on the purity of the soul in which it is beheld. Originally, God created man perfectly pure and undefiled, so that man could clearly reveal the divine image, not as an empty silhouette, but as a true and living image of the invisible God, revealing the likeness of His inward, hidden, and unutterable beauty. This likeness was revealed in various aspects of man's nature: God's wisdom in man's *understanding*; God's goodness, gentleness and patience in man's *character*; God's divine love and mercy in the *affections* of man's heart; God's righteousness, holiness, justice and purity in the *will* of man. God's longsuffering and truth in the *words and actions* of man; and God's authority and power in man's *dominion* over the earth and everything in it.

From the divine image implanted in him, man should have gained knowledge both of God and of himself. Man might have understood that God, his Creator, is the all in all, the Supreme Being, from whom all created beings derive their existence, and in whom, and by whom, all things that are and subsist. He might also have recognised that he, in essence, was but an image or representation of God, who is alone the essence of love, the source of life, and the embodiment of holiness. Since any goodness in man is but a reflection of God's perfect and infinite goodness, all worship, praise, honour, and glory should be ascribed to Him alone, as no other being possesses these qualities.

Man should also have realised the profound difference between himself and the Divine. Man is not God, but rather God's *image* and as such, he ought to represent nothing but God in character. As God's portrait, the purpose of man's existence was to reveal and glorify God alone. Nothing else should be revealed in man's thoughts, will, desires, emotions, words, or actions. If anything else or any other spirit motivates or influences man, he ceases to be the image of God and he becomes the image of something else. If anyone would become and remain the image of God, they must completely surrender themselves to God, and submit entirely to His will. They must allow God to work in them as He pleases, without any reservation denying their own will to do the will of our Heavenly Father. In this way, they become a holy instrument in God's hands, doing His will and His work. Those who have surrendered to God do not pursue their own will, but the will of God; they do not love themselves, but God; they do not seek their own honour but the honour of God. They are not driven by a desire for wealth, status, or possessions, but instead recognize that all good things come from God, and being content to possess God alone, rise above all these things. By letting go of their love for themselves and the world, they become fully dependent on God and allow Him to be all in them and to work in them by His Holy Spirit.

This is what the perfect innocence, purity, and holiness of man consisted of at creation. Adam came forth from the hand of God a grown man yet as a simple child, full of sincere love, joy, peace of mind, light and life, completely surrendered to God's guidance and direction. One in whom self-love, self-honour, self-exaltation, self-confidence, self-assurance, self-sufficiency and self-righteousness had not yet germinated. There is no greater innocence than for one to freely permit our heavenly Father to work in oneself as He pleases. There is no greater purity than for one to do the will of God, without reservation. There is no greater holiness than to become an instrument in the hands of the Holy God.

As a consequence of being filled with the spirit of God (John 3:34), our Lord Jesus Christ, during his time on earth, was a perfect example of this complete devotion to God's will. He sacrificed His own will to God His Father, in blameless obedience, humility, and meekness. He deprived Himself of all honour, self-esteem, self-interest, self-love, self-pleasure and joy, and allowed God to think, speak and act in and through him. Jesus made God's will and pleasure His own, as the Father Himself testified from Heaven: "This is my beloved Son, in whom I am well pleased" (Mat 3:17).

Jesus Christ is the true image of God, in whom nothing appears but God alone and those things that characterise His nature: love, mercy, long-suffering, patience, meekness, gentleness, righteousness, holiness. By Him the invisible God was willing to be discovered and made known to man. But He is the image of God in a more sublime sense, as in Him shines the infinite splendour of uncreated light (Heb 1:3), having divinity in Himself and being the express image of his Father's glory. But our focus here is not the divinity of Christ, but rather His humanity as He lived and interacted with people on earth.

Adam should have preserved the spirit and holy innocence in which the image of God was originally bestowed upon him, in humility and obedience. However, becoming self-important, he failed to recognize that he was only a living mirror, created for the purpose of reflecting the divine nature. Becoming captive to his own self-interest, he put himself before God, severing his relationship with God, from where the divine image in him originated and by which it was maintained. The spirit of God being withdrawn from him, the spirit of self-love, self-will, self-honour, self-interest, self-confidence, self-sufficiency, self-justification and self-righteousness took control of his soul. God would no longer be man's sole glory, honour, confidence, righteousness and praise.

Man should also have learned that having the image of God is what unites him to God and that it is only in this union that true and everlasting rest, peace, joy, life, and happiness are found. He should have realised that when this union is broken he suffers from a restless mind and a vexed spirit. He then ceases to be the image of God, and turning from God to material things, he loses access to the eternal good that comes from God alone.

Chapter 2: The Fall of Man.

As by one man's disobedience many were made sinners, so by the obedience of one shall many be made righteous. – Rom 5:19

Despite being numbered among the sons of God, having come forth perfect from the hands of the Almighty, and being the most glorious object in all creation, man was not content with his privileged position. This rebellion against God first arose subconsciously in the heart before being manifest in the deliberate act of eating the forbidden fruit. In seeking escape from their dependence on God, the Self-Existent one (1 Tim 6:16), and to exalt themselves to be as god, they displaced their creator and robbed Him of the honour that was due to Him alone.

The fall of Adam and Eve, as manifested in their disobedience, was a direct result of turning away from God to themselves. In thinking that he could get along fine without God and turning away from him, Adam essentially said to God's Holy Spirit within himself, "Go thy way for this time; when I have a convenient season, I will call for thee." (Acts 24:25). Tragically, Adam failed to realise the grave consequences of rejecting the Holy Spirit for which man's flesh had been designed to be a dwelling place (1 Cor 6:19). As Jesus explained in a parable, our bodies cannot remain vacant, for as soon as they are not occupied by the Holy Spirit, unclean spirits will inevitably invade and possess them. Immediately upon the eviction of the Holy Spirit from man, the unclean spirit of self-justification possessed Adam's soul along "with seven other spirits more wicked than himself" (Luke 11:24-26).

It is not as pagan philosophers and their acolytes suppose that the spirit of man remained good while his physical body became evil. After his fall, Adam's body became no more evil than that of all that is flesh upon the earth, such as that of cattle or other animals. But it became subject to sickness and decay and accustomed to evil, whereas before it had only known good. It is the spirit within man that sets him apart from all other flesh and which, at the fall, become predominantly evil. It is the unclean spirit that possessed man that brings death; the literal flesh is of little account (John 6:63). Many misinterpret Jesus' words, "the spirit indeed is willing but the flesh is weak," (Mat 26:41) and infer that He was affirming the pagan concept of the soul.

The Fall of Man

Instead, the Bible affirms that weakness of the body is not inherently evil (1 Cor 2:3-5; 2 Cor 12:9-10; Phil 4:12-13). Remembering that the word flesh is not just a reference to the physical body but the psyche, we see that it is the psyche of man that became enslaved to the unclean spirits of selfishness and pride at the fall.

When, as the result of Adam's fall, the spirit of God departed from man, he lost the divine image, the righteousness, wisdom and holiness he had originally possessed. Having lost the heavenly, spiritual and divine qualities that were once his, he became earthly, sensual and brutish. His understanding was darkened, he became spiritually blind, his will became stubborn and perverse, and all the faculties of his soul were entirely alienated from God. In essence, Adam's original sin was no different from Lucifer's original sin, who also sought to free himself from his creator. It constitutes the most abominable and detestable of all possible sins, and produced the same evil result. Having committed the same sin as Lucifer, having rebelled against the majesty of heaven, Adam became inwardly like Satan himself, bearing his likeness in his heart. Losing the divine image, he took up the image of the Devil. He was no longer an instrument in the hands of God, but an instrument of Satan, capable of every kind of diabolical wickedness. Man therefore conceived hostility toward God and developed a disposition to dispose of Him. Instead of bearing God's Holy Spirit, he took on the spirit of devils. Man became a hold of every foul spirit and a cage of every filthy and hateful bird (Isa 13:21; Rev 18:2).

We need to deeply examine and understand the fall of Adam and the true nature of Adam and Eve's sin and recognise it in ourselves, for its infection is greater, deeper and more deadly than words can express or be conceived in thought. "Know yourself!" and consider what you are: a creature fallen from the image of God which has become an image of Satan, embodying all his wicked tendencies, ungodliness, character and the very nature of the Devil himself. While man was originally created with a heavenly nature and endowed with the Holy Spirit, since the fall man carries within himself an unclean spirit and an earthly, carnal, and corrupt nature. By means of deceitful words the devil succeeded in sowing in Adam's soul the seed of the serpent: the hateful seed of self-love, self-will, self-interest, self-sufficiency, self-righteousness, self-exaltation, and the ambition of being like God. This seed, rooted in Adam's self-love and disobedience, contains the entire image of Satan with all its characteristics and has through the law of heredity, passed to all his descendants. Just as a natural seed contains the blueprint for every feature of the future plant, this seed contains the potential for all the evils that sprout from it.

The Almighty, addressing the serpent, said, "I will put enmity between thee and the woman and between thy seed and her seed" (Gen. 3:15). If the seed of the woman refers to Jesus Christ, then the seed of the serpent can only refer to those who crucify Christ by their sins. As all seeds produce fruit, the seed of the serpent produces its own evil fruit, namely the image of Satan in the children of Belial. This is why Christ referred to the self-righteous Pharisees as "children of the devil" (John 8:44), and those who are consumed by self-love as "a generation of vipers" (Mat 3:7) and even called the self-confident Simon Peter, "Satan" (John 6:70), and so all those who are proud and devilish are the seed of the serpent: a manifestation of Satan himself. This evil has been passed down to all mankind, so that we are born spiritually dead, making us children of wrath and damnation unless Jesus Christ redeems us from this miserable state.

From the serpent's dreadful seed comes a deformed and foul image, which grows and develops without needing to be fed by outward temptations and the corruption of others. We can observe this corruption manifesting itself in children from their earliest years in self-will and disobedience. As they grow older, these traits give rise to selfishness, ambition, and a desire for self-exaltation: worldly glory, love of applause, love of pleasure, vengefulness and a tendency to deceive. These evils multiply and soon lead to vanity, arrogance, pride, quarrelling, blasphemy, cursing, fraud, infidelity, contempt of God and His Holy Word, wrath, hatred and envy, revenge and murder, and all kinds of cruelty. As various circumstances present themselves, they will exhibit other vices, such as self-indulgence, lust, an evil imagination, and obscene communications and gestures. They may develop an inclination for drunkenness, rioting, and other forms of intemperance. Additionally, they may display covetousness, extortion, and other sinful behaviours that are so many and varied that it is impossible to list them all.

The prophet Jeremiah aptly describes the human heart as "deceitful above all things" and "desperately wicked," (Jer 17:9) making it impossible to fully comprehend its depths of corruption. And to all this we can add: idolaters, mockers, lovers of darkness, false apostles, deceitful workers transforming themselves into the apostles of Christ (2 Cor 11:13), teachers of false Christs and false gospels, other spirits, perverters of the Scriptures, deniers of the faith and haters of the truth. We must also acknowledge the unpardonable sin of grieving away the Holy Spirit by persistently refusing to repent. All this is but the image of Satan and the fruits of the serpent's seed sown in man. It is difficult to imagine that a helpless and seemingly innocent child can contain such a depth of wickedness and corruption. However, this is precisely what we see. Who could possibly have believed that the imaginations of man's thoughts are "only evil continually" if it was not that man chooses from his childhood to express them in words and actions what would otherwise be concealed as in a seed (Gen 6:5; 8:21).

It is easy to recognise the unclean spirit that lurks within man waiting to manifest itself in coarse, uncivilised or unseemly behaviour. More insidious, however, is the evil that subtly cloaks itself in a veneer of goodness: works of charity, moralism, and even good intentions. Even the supposedly good things that an unregenerate man does with good intentions ultimately serve an evil purpose. As the scripture says "but we are all as an unclean thing, and all our righteousness's are as filthy rags" (Isa 64:6). Saul's misguided persecution of the Christians before his conversion, thinking he was doing God's will, is a good example of this (Acts 8:1-3).

The corruption of man is so complete that, notwithstanding appearances, it is impossible for unregenerate man to do any good whatsoever. "Who can bring a clean thing out of an unclean? Not one." (Job 14:4). "Can the Ethiopian change his skin or the leopard his spots? Then may ye also do good, that are accustomed to do evil" (Jer 13:23). The apostle explains "so then they that are in the flesh cannot please God" but adds that it is not necessary to live according to the flesh, with its unclean spirit, its vain imaginations and darkened understanding, but that God has made a way for man to be renewed in spirit, and become a new creature in the image of Christ (Rom 8:8-11; Eph. 4:23, 24; 1 Pet 4:6).

In placing enmity between Christ and the serpent's seed, God opened the door to the possibility that man, being repulsed by what he had become, might choose to be restored to the image of God. In the heart of all except the most hardened sinners, there is a longing after good: being the divine influence of the Holy Spirit upon their consciences. Just as, prior to his fall, Adam was not immune from the influence of evil spirits, afterwards he was not immune from the influence of the Holy Spirit. If the first was not the case, he never would not have fallen, and if the second was not so, no one could ever be saved. So man may actively choose to expel the unclean spirit that possesses his soul and be restored to righteousness by the indwelling of the Holy Spirit.

He who in this life rejects the grace of God and accordingly fails to correct this corruption of nature by being truly transformed and renewed in Christ Jesus, will retain this satanic nature forever. His pride and selfishness: self-love, self-will, self-confidence, self-interest, self-indulgence and self-righteousness will never depart from him. Christ will declare, "he that is holy, let him be holy still and he which is filthy, let him be filthy still" (Rev. 22:11). Having neglected the opportunity for purification in this life, he will bear the image of Satan together with him in the lake of fire. "For without are dogs and sorcerers, and whosoever loveth and maketh a lie" (Rev. 21:8; 22:15).

Chapter 3. How Man Is Restored In Christ

In Christ Jesus neither circumcision availeth anything, nor uncircumcision, but a new creature. – Gal. 6:15.

As fallen beings, our nature is miserably depraved, desperately perverted and corrupted in all its aspects. As a result, it is absolutely essential that it be purified and renewed. Our soul must undergo a complete renovation, involving all its powers and faculties. But how can this occur? Since our nature is fundamentally corrupted by supreme evil (God's absence) only a vital infusion of Himself (the supreme Good) can restore and renew it, making it again like Himself.

The regeneration by which a sinner is made righteous, a child of perdition becomes a child of grace, and a son of Belial becomes a son of God, is called the new birth and described as receiving a new spirit, heart and mind from Christ. The apostle Paul, says it is being "renewed in the spirit of our mind," "putting off the old man," and being "transformed into the image of God." He likewise describes it as being "renewed in knowledge after the image of him that created us," and "the renewing of the Holy Ghost." (Eph. 4:23; Col. 3:10; Tit. 3:5; Eze. 11:19).

The new birth is not a work that man can do for himself. It is not choosing to believe in Christ, or "coming to Christ." It is not mental assent to dogma, nor working up a feeling, nor self-identifying as a Christian, nor being accepted into church membership, nor undertaking the rite of baptism nor the manifestation of some special ability. It is also not the transformation of the outer man; it is not turning away from certain sins or choosing to obey God. It is not a moral improvement of oneself, nor a new disposition nor a change of behaviour. All these man may do, and often does, on his own. These things may precede or follow the new birth but they are not the new birth itself. A person might do all these things but unless they are a new creation, they are as it were, sewing new patches onto old garments or putting new wine into old bottles which is of no value (Mat 9:16-17). The new birth is also not just a metaphor or a figure of speech, or change in one's heavenly status, or a mystical phenomenon, but a real and profound inward transformation that is worthy of the majesty and power of an omnipotent God. It is absurd to think, as some do, that almighty God is unable in this life, to conceive in the souls of men a new man in the image of Christ, created in righteousness and true holiness (Eph 4:24).

The new birth occurs when the carnal spirit of man is dispossessed and the Holy Spirit takes control of the inner man, radically transforming it. This transformation encompasses the inner workings of the mind (our psyche), both conscious and unconscious, including our thoughts, feelings, desires, impulses, inclinations, priorities, motivations and values that drive our actions and decisions and is revealed in words and actions.

This is what the scripture means when it commands us to put off the old man that a new man may arise (Col 3:9, 10; Eph 4:22, 24; Rom 6:6). No one can of themselves dethrone the unclean spirit that rules their entire being. Only the Holy Spirit can depose the carnal spirit, and purge the inner man from everything that defiles it. The unclean spirit of self-will, self-love, self-interest, self-esteem, self-indulgence, self-honour, self-confidence and self-sufficiency is banished and a holy spirit of repentance: humility, meekness, contrition and godly dependence takes its place. The fruit of this change is seen in fruits of repentance: namely self-abasement, self-sacrifice, self-denial, self-renunciation, self-distrust, submission to God and a continual dependence on Him. Unless this transformation takes place, man can never escape his iniquity and an image of Satan can never become an image of God.

This transformation is a threefold process: first, by the Holy Spirit, as Jesus spoke of being "born of the Spirit" (John 3:5). Secondly, by faith, as the scripture says, "whosoever believeth that Jesus is the Christ is born of God" (1 John 5:1). Thirdly, by repentance, as Christ said, "Except a man be born of water and of the Spirit, he cannot enter into the kingdom of God" (John 3:5). Being born of water, or baptism, is a symbol of repentance as the scripture says, "I indeed baptize you with water unto repentance" (Mat 3:11 see also Acts 13:24). The new birth is first conceived in us by the word of the God, which is the seed of the new creation: for we are "born again, not of corruptible seed, but of incorruptible, by the word of God, which liveth and abideth forever." (1 Pet 1:23). And, again, "Of his own will begat he us with the word of truth, that we should be a kind of first-fruits of his creatures." (Jam 1:18). This seed is watered and made to germinate in our hearts by the Holy Spirit. It is through the Holy Spirit that the goodness and holiness of God, as revealed in the word of God, shines forth dispelling our spiritual darkness and transforming our knowledge of ourselves and understanding of our true nature. This produces in us faith, which, grasping the word of God, embraces Christ who gives us repentance (Acts 5:31; 2 Tim 2:25) and we are born again.

In reference to this work of regeneration, Christ is called "the everlasting Father" (Isa. 9:6) not only because repentance comes from Christ (Acts 5:31), but because the regeneration of man must proceed from the incarnation of the Son of God. To restore those who are born of the flesh and subject to its bondage and make them to be partakers of the divine nature, it was necessary for Christ to become flesh. As the Scripture says: "For what the law could not do, in that it was weak through the flesh, God sending his own Son in the likeness of sinful flesh, and for sin, condemned sin in the flesh: That the righteousness of the law might be fulfilled in us, who walk not after the flesh, but after the Spirit" (Rom 8:3-4), that is, Christ has made it possible for us to be restored to righteousness by being born again of, and continuing to be filled with, the Spirit of God, as He was. (John 3:8). When the scripture says that "Christ his own self bare our sins in his own body on the tree, that we, being dead to sins, should live unto righteousness" (1 Peter 2:24), it does not just mean that Christ bore our guilt, but that Christ bore the corruption of human nature, the sinfulness of man, in His own body and defeated it in Himself upon the tree. In dying to sin and self, He fully destroyed the image of Satan and opened the way for man to be born again to a new life free from sin, and become the servant of righteousness (Rom 6:18).

It was by rejecting the carnal spirit of His humanity so that instead "the Spirit of the Lord should rest upon him, the spirit of wisdom and understanding, the spirit of counsel and might, the spirit of knowledge and of the fear of the Lord" (Isa. 11:2), that Christ overcame the corruption of His flesh and cleansed and sanctified it (Heb 4:15): "and being made perfect, he became the author of eternal salvation unto all them that obey him" (Heb 5:9). For us to become new creatures, in Him, by Him, and through Him, we must likewise reject our own carnal spirits and receive from Christ the spirit of wisdom and understanding in place of our natural blindness and the spirit of the fear of the Lord, instead of the spirit of disobedience and faithlessness.

Since man turned from God to himself becoming ambitious, proud, self-confident, self-sufficient and disobedient, so his rebellion could not be purged and washed away, except by the Son of God turning away from himself to God and emptying himself (Phil 2:7, margin), becoming humble, lowly, self-surrendered, and obedient. And as Christ, in profound humility when in His carnal nature upon earth, turned from Himself to God, so it is necessary, that He should be the same in you; that He should dwell in your soul, and in the same way restore the image of God in you. We must live in the new birth, and the new birth in us; we must be in Christ, and Christ in us; we must live in the spirit of Christ, and the spirit of Christ in us (Gal. 2:20).

In Christ, we see the perfect pattern of the new man regenerated in God's image. His life is a reflection of God's character, the fleshly Adam having no dominion. God set Christ before our eyes that by contemplating Him and His righteous life, we might be daily more and more renewed in His image. Consider therefore the humble, obedient, and patient Jesus Christ and learn of Him; live as He lived; live in Him, and tread in His steps. Jesus took our flesh and came to live on this earth being conceived by the Holy Ghost to show us what it means to be born of the spirit: to be your example, your mirror, and the rule of your life. He only is the rule of life and the pattern that every Christian should strive to imitate. There is but one example, Christ, and the apostles unanimously set Him before us to imitate. He is our example in all things as we read "for even hereunto were ye called: because Christ also suffered for us, leaving us an example, that ye should follow his steps" (1Pet 2:21) and we are to view His life, death, and resurrection in the same manner. We should die unto to sin and self with Him, and spiritually rise again, and walk in newness of life in Him, with Him, and by Him, "even as he also walked." (Rom. 6:4). And as we walk as He did, despising the corruption and weakness of our flesh and humbly pleading with the Father to be emptied of ourselves and filled with His Spirit and the will and strength to do His pleasure, (Phil 2:13; 2 Cor 3:5) we shall overcome our carnal nature even as He did. (Rev 3:21).

Every true Christian is born twice: first a physical birth "after the flesh" and secondly a spiritual birth "after the spirit." The first is from beneath: carnal and earthly, while the second is from above heavenly and holy. The first birth makes one to be spiritually dead in his own sins; the second birth makes one to be alive unto righteousness in Christ. The first birth is propagated by the first Adam, through the seed of the serpent, and produces the image of the devil. The second birth is propagated by the second Adam, Christ, forming the image of God by the Holy Spirit. As a result, every Christian has two distinct lines of descent: a fleshly lineage from Adam and a spiritual lineage from Christ. This means that there are two "men" living within one person. The first natural born "old man" and the second "new man" born of the Holy Spirit. The first seeks its own interests being concerned with material things and external appearances, the second seeks the interests of God, being concerned with spiritual things and internal realities.

From Adam we inherit a carnal spirit, which is proud, arrogant, covetous, presumptuous, blasphemous, ungrateful, disobedient, violent, impatient, rash, wrathful, vengeful, hateful, seeking only to benefit oneself at the expense of others, unchaste, unclean, fickle, indulgent, slanderous, deceitful, foolish, blind, mad, cowardly, brutish, earthly, and defies the wrath of God. However, from Christ, we can receive the Holy Spirit, which is humble, meek, upright, faithful, pleasing to God, obedient, gentle, modest, long-suffering, loving, merciful, forgiving, good, compassionate, generous, mild, chaste, pure, temperate, wise, understanding, truthful, bold, constant, honest, heavenly, divine, and serves God acceptably with reverence and godly fear (Heb 12:28). The carnal spirit is a despot that keeps us in slavery to the desires of the flesh, but the Holy Spirit sets us free from its bondage. "Now the Lord is that Spirit: and where the Spirit of the Lord is, there is liberty" (2Cor 3:17).

The carnal spirit and the Holy Spirit of God war against each other in the soul of a man who has been born again as the scripture says, "but as then he that was born after the flesh persecuted him that was born after the Spirit, even so it is now" (Gal 4:29) and "the flesh lusteth against the Spirit, and the Spirit against the flesh: and these are contrary the one to the other" (Gal 5:17). The apostle Paul further explains this warfare "I delight in the law of God after the inward man: but I see another law in my members, warring against the law of my mind." (Rom 7:22-23) and "the weapons of our warfare are not carnal, but mighty through God to the pulling down of strong holds; Casting down imaginations, and every high thing that exalteth itself against the knowledge of God, and bringing into captivity every thought to the obedience of Christ" (2 Cor 10:4-5).

This warfare against the carnal spirit is, however, not one of merely going through the motions but requires constant watchfulness and effort, lest the unclean spirit reassert itself (Mat 12:43-45). "I therefore so run, not as uncertainly; so fight I, not as one that beateth the air: But I keep under my body, and bring it into subjection: lest that by any means, when I have preached to others, I myself should be a castaway" (1 Cor 9:26 – 27). And only those who, through the power of the Holy Spirit, mortify the unclean spirit of their flesh and its evil fruit are truly born again. "For if ye live after the flesh, ye shall die: but if ye through the Spirit do mortify the deeds of the body, ye shall live." (Rom 8:13).

Whatever corruptions we inherit from Adam must be overcome in Christ. In His humility, our pride and ambition must be crucified; in beholding His poverty, our desires for earthly things must fade away. The contemplation of His suffering and the insults He endured should subdue our lusts; the reproaches He endured and His entire resignation to submit to the world's contempt should restrain us from chasing worldly honours and indulging in anger and passion. Whoever lives in Christ by the Spirit has put on the new man and all its accompanying graces. Their meekness and obedience are the meekness and obedience of Christ; their patience and humility are the patience and humility of Christ; and their life itself is the life of Christ, as they live by and in Him. This is the "new creature" which is created in the image of God (2 Cor. 5:17); and that life of Christ in us, of which the apostle Paul says by experience, "I live, yet not I, but Christ liveth in me." (Gal. 2:20). This is what it really means to follow Christ, to walk in the light of His life, and to bring forth "fruits meet for repentance;" (Mat 3:8). This is the way that the "old man" is destroyed, the carnal life gradually declines, and the new and divine life takes root in the soul. He who has this life is not a nominal Christian, but a real one; a Christian not in word and in appearance only, but in deed and in truth. He is a true child of God, begotten of Him, revived and transformed by faith after the image of Jesus Christ

Christ's death and resurrection was the culmination of His victory over His corrupt mortal flesh. Throughout the New Testament, the apostles lay the foundation of repentance and new life solely upon Christ's victory. Jesus Himself explained: "Thus it behoved Christ to suffer, and to rise from the dead the third day: and that repentance and remission of sins should be preached in his name" (Luke 24:46, 47). Having overcome the corruption that is in the world and restored the divine nature in human flesh, Christ offers us the same victory (2 Pet 1:4). He invites us to overcome even as He overcame (Rev 3:21). As the apostle Peter writes, "God hath begotten us again unto a lively hope by the resurrection of Jesus Christ from the dead" (1 Pet 1:3).

Without Christ making a way to overcome the corruption within man, feelings of remorse or regret are powerless to bring about change in man, and at most could only result in sin being overlooked. Since Christ has now opened the way to a regenerate life, repentance combined with faith, obtains for us forgiveness and becomes the catalyst for the transformation of our nature, restoring us into the image of God.

Chapter 4. Repentance the Key to Redemption

I tell you..., except ye repent, ye shall all likewise perish. – Luke 13:3

If any man will come after me, let him deny himself, and take up his cross daily, and follow me. – Luke 9:23.

God takes pleasure in showing mercy and forgiving sinners, He says "My heart is troubled for him; I will surely have mercy on him, says the Lord." (Hos 11:8; also Jer 31:20). It is for this reason that Christ shed His blood. (1 Cor. 8:11). The redemption accomplished for man by Christ's sacrifice is incredibly powerful, extensive and effective, so that every soul who truly desires it can be, not just forgiven, but also fully restored to the image of God. However, this can only take place if the sinner truly desires to be restored and seeks for it as the most priceless treasure in this life until it is obtained. This desire for restoration, rather than just forgiveness, is contrary to the flesh and it must be instilled in man by God. This is what the Bible means when it says, He "gives repentance... and forgiveness of sins" (Acts 5:31); in other words, for Christ's sake, God awakens in man the longing to be restored, pardons his wrongdoing and transforms him into a new creature. It is only when this happens that the death of Christ becomes truly effective and there is joy in heaven (Luke 15:7).

By the fall of Adam, man became earthly, carnal, and devilish; without God and without love: since being without God, he was also without love. Man turned from the love of God to the love of himself and the world. Man now only seeks his own interests, pleasure, honour and glory; he defends, flatters, and applauds himself. In seeking to set himself up, as it were, into a god, Adam plunged himself and all his posterity into an awful sin and depravity. This depravity must be entirely rooted out and this can only be done by a profound repentance: godly sorrow and the crucifixion of the flesh.

True repentance, or true conversion, is not just self-interested remorse or regret out of fear that our sins have provoked the wrath of God against ourselves. Godly sorrow is not rooted in self-pity, nor focused on one's own feelings or reputation. It looks instead beyond individual sins to the underlying sinful nature that caused them. It is the work of the Holy Spirit, which, out of love for God and all that is good, leads us to recognise and despise our depravity and sinfulness in view of God's hatred of sin. Then, earnestly mourning over our woeful condition, and understanding through the Gospel the mercy of God towards the humble and contrite soul, and longing to be restored to holiness, we confess our sinfulness and, by faith in Christ Jesus, we earnestly seek to be saved from it.

Repentance is not about cleaning up the outside of the cup while ignoring the inside (Mat 23:25-27). Repentance is not only turning away from gross and open sins but also searching into the hidden recesses of our minds and confronting the sin that lurks there. It will not do to pull the evil fruit off a corrupt tree (Mat 7:17-19) and attach good fruit to its branches; the entire tree must be rooted up (Matt 12:33). Since sin arises from within ourselves, (Jam 1:15) repentance must begin with a turning away from of our inner self: our spirit, thoughts, desires and feelings, from which our words and actions arise. Repentance is the crucifying of the old man (Rom 6:6). The apostle Paul, tells us to "Put off... the old man which is corrupt according to the deceitful lusts; and be renewed in the spirit of your mind; and put on the new man, which after God is created in righteousness and true holiness." (Eph. 4:22-24). Repentance is a turning away from the root cause of our sin, our self-interest, self-love and self-sufficiency, and having a broken and contrite heart that has surrendered to God its self-esteem and self-confidence.

While not all bear the same evil fruit of sin, not all are thieves, or adulterers, or blasphemers, or Sabbath-breakers etc., all have the same evil root of sin deep within them. This is why, "God commands all people everywhere to repent" (Acts 17:30), not just the unbelieving or unchurched. All must be converted from a love of themselves to the love of God; from the love of the material things to the love of the spiritual things; from the love of display and pleasure to the love of the humility and self-denial of Christ.

It is only in the light of Christ's infinite goodness, righteousness and holiness that we can grasp the stark reality of the profound corruption of our soul that disguises itself in seemingly innocent thoughts, feelings and desires. Repentance is the horror and sorrow we experience when we recognise within our self the image of Satan, and long after the image of God. As when Job, having seen the Lord, said, "I abhor myself and repent in dust and ashes," (Job 42:5-6) or when Isaiah saw the Lord of Hosts "high and lifted up" and said,

True Christianity

"Woe is me! For I am undone; because I am a man of unclean lips." (Isa 6:5). Repentance is to despise and mourn over the seed of the serpent that is embedded deep within our soul and fall at Jesus' feet pleading for grace to escape its power.

Repentance can only occur after an encounter with Jesus when we see Him, as it were, face to face. Just as no man can by searching find out God (Job 11:7) unless God reveals Himself to him (Matt 11:27), so too, can no man can repent of himself: for repentance is the gift of God (Acts 5:31; 2 Tim 2:25). A man may feel remorse or regret of himself, but only those who have received a knowledge of the holiness of God (Rom 2:4), and, as a consequence, a true knowledge of themselves, can repent. This knowledge can only be obtained as God reveals it to man. Only as God reveals to us the deep and secret things that are within our own selves by His Spirit (Dan 2:22; Luke 10:21; 1 Cor 2:10) can we truly repent. God will not give us this gift of self-knowledge and repentance unless we desire it. He says "Ask, and it shall be given you; seek, and ye shall find; knock, and it shall be opened unto you" (Matt 7:7) "and ye shall seek me, and find me, when ye shall search for me with all your heart." (Jer 29:13). And if we truly are Christ's disciples we will seek His face anew every day and seeking to be emptied of self and filled with his spirit, we will every day repent over the evil within us, which is to say, we will be crucified to the world (Ga 6:14), to the desires of the eyes and flesh, and to the pride of life every day.

The crucifixion of the old man, with its desires and pleasures, is necessary for the resurrection of the new man in Christ by the quickening of the spirit. In repentance, the old Adam, with his corrupt nature, dies within us, and Christ is resurrected in us by faith (Gal 2:20). The two are inseparable: the resurrection of the spirit follows the mortification of the flesh, and the destruction of the old man is the life and resurrection of the new man. "Though our outward man perish, yet the inward man is renewed day by day." (2 Cor. 4:16). We are, therefore, called to "reckon ourselves to be dead indeed unto sin, but alive unto God, through Jesus Christ our Lord" (Rom. 6:11).

"The crucifixion of the flesh" is not about physical self-harm, or denying ourselves sleep or clothing or food and water, or shutting ourselves away from society, but about putting to death the carnal spirit within us and its manifestation in our lives. According to Jesus, the things that defile man come from within him (Mark 7:20-23), meaning that the evil we do proceeds from the unclean spirit that is within us. This is also why Jesus said, "It is the spirit that quickeneth; the flesh profiteth nothing" (Joh 6:63), highlighting that the flesh is under the control of the spirit within man, and that discomforting our bodies is of no profit. This unclean spirit is what man must empty himself from. In calling for crucifying the flesh, the apostle mentions, not only "the deeds of the body" (Rom 8:13), but, specifically, integral parts of our psyche; "mortify your... fornication, uncleanness, inordinate affection, evil concupiscence, and covetousness" (Col 3:5). Crucifying the flesh is as much about eradicating "the works of the flesh" (Gal 5:19-22), as it is about putting to death the carnal spirit within.

Therefore, a man must deny himself (Luke 9:23), that is, he must mortify his own will and allow himself to be led entirely by God's will. He must stop loving, seeking, and esteeming himself, instead considering himself to be the most unworthy and miserable of all creatures. He must surrender himself and give up everything he has for the love of Christ and reject the world's display and vanity. He must set aside his own wisdom and talents and being blind to these trust in God alone. He must even "hate his own life" (Luke 14:26), which means despising his carnal mind with its pleasures: his pride, covetousness, lust, wrath, and envy, He must give up his self-interest, self-honour, self-confidence, self-sufficiency. He must not please himself, but rather displease himself, and not attribute anything good to his own strength or ability. This is what it means to crucify our own flesh with its desires and inclinations (Gal 5:24). This, and this alone, is that true repentance and mortification of the flesh without which no man can ever be a disciple of Jesus Christ. This only is conversion from self, the world, and the devil, unto God (Acts 26:18); without which no one can obtain freedom from sin, nor be saved. This repentance is what it means to be "always bearing about in the body the dying of the Lord Jesus that the life also of Jesus might be made manifest in our body." (2Cor 4:10). It is the fruit of Christ's passion in us, leading us by this sincere repentance to die to sin and self that Christ may live in us and we in Him. All this is necessary to transform man into a new creature in Christ Jesus, without which nothing is of any value in God's sight (2 Cor 5:17; Gal 6:15).

Those who think that the cross of Christ is the tribulations and afflictions of this life are greatly mistaken. The true cross that we are called to bear after our Lord daily is inward repentance and the emptying of ourselves through the mortification of the desires and tendencies of our flesh. We must submit to our enemies with great patience and overcome the malice of slanderers by humility and mildness, following the example of the Lamb of God, who made himself of no reputation and renounced all worldly splendour and glory, and everything that is commonly esteemed great and noble. By bearing this cross, a person truly dies to the world. This is the true yoke of Christ, which the Saviour spoke about when He said; "Take my yoke upon you, and learn from me; for I am meek and lowly in heart" (Mat 11:29). This means that we must remove our self-love and ambition by earnest inward humility, just as we see in Jesus' example. We must also subdue our urge for self-justification by following His example of meekness. This is an easy yoke and a light burden for the new man, but it is bitter and painful to the flesh.

This yoke of Christ is not about adopting a set of rules and regulations for life nor retreating to monasteries or cloisters. While the heart remains disordered and corrupt, and a person is puffed up with spiritual pride and a pharisaic contempt for others, they have not died to the world but still live for it. This is not the Christian yoke nor is it the cross of Christ because these consist of mortifying the desires of the flesh and its sinful tendencies; in turning away from the world to God; in living a daily life of inward and constant sorrow for our sinfulness; in a daily dying to the world and living to Christ by faith; in following His steps with sincere lowliness and humility; and in confiding only in the mercy of God in Christ Jesus.

But certain and obvious as these truths are in themselves, there are many that call themselves Christians who have no real repentance, and who yet will presume to lay claim to a share in the merits of Christ and in the remission of sins which He has purchased. Jesus Christ declared, "Those who are well have no need for a physician, but those who are sick do. I came not to call the righteous but sinners to repentance." (Mat 9:12-13). Jesus teaches us that He calls sinners, not primarily to accept religious beliefs and practices, but to be transformed by lifelong repentance. It is not the symptoms of a carnal spirit that Jesus wants to treat, but the underlying corruption of spirit. He calls sinners not just to feel sorry for having sinned and attempt to compensate through works of charity, devotion or the law, but through godly sorrow, to give up their carnal spirit and its works of the mind and body that lead to spiritual death, obtaining freedom from sin through faith, and living a righteous life in Christ. This is what the Bible calls "repentance from dead works" (Heb 6:1). Unless we experience this kind of repentance, the benefits and merit of Christ's sacrifice are of no use to us.

Just as a powerful medicine can have no effect unless patients stop doing things that harm their health and prevent the medication from working, so too, Christ's blood and sacrifice are useless to someone who refuses to completely give up their carnal spirit and its sinful habits of thought and action and live according to the gospel. As Paul says, "Those who do such things" (the works of the flesh) "shall not inherit the kingdom of God," and therefore have no part in the Lord Jesus Christ (Gal. 5:21). For Christ's precious blood to heal us, we must first recognise our spiritual disease and feel the urgent need for healing. "Those who are well have no need for a physician, but those who are sick" (Mat 9:12).

A person who is conscious of their spiritual disease, not only feels genuine contrition for its symptoms, manifested in their thoughts and actions, but over its underlying cause. They sense that unless they are fully healed, it will ultimately lead to their eternal death. The physician of souls only accepts patients who are genuinely concerned about their spiritual wellbeing, care about their past lives and future wellbeing and are willing to avoid worldly desires, honours, riches and vanity. It is only those who are broken in heart and contrite in spirit, only those who fervently desire and thirst after righteousness no matter the cost, who are in a condition to receive the transforming influence of Jesus' blood, death, and redemption. Patients without this attitude cannot be cured; not recognizing their sorry condition, they have no need of a doctor. In this case, their faith is meaningless as Christ cannot help them and His redemption has no saving effect on their soul.

Our blessed Lord has called us to this genuine repentance, this true and inward conversion from the world to God. The imputation of His righteousness, along with the freedom from our sins, apprehended by faith, is promised to those who experience this repentance alone. If we are lacking in repentance, Christ will profit us nothing, and we cannot become partakers of His grace and favour, nor of the efficacy of His merits. These can only be received by a contrite, penitent, lowly, and believing heart.

Unless we learn the true nature of repentance, we will fall into the common mistake of thinking that repentance is simply giving up obvious sins such as theft, fornication, or profanity. While this may be a kind of external repentance, the Scriptures clearly emphasize the importance of inward repentance which consumes the entire soul. A person who experiences true repentance not only has good behaviour, but also denies and hates themselves. They renounce the world and all they have and crucify their flesh and commit themselves by faith to God alone, offering up to Him a broken and contrite heart as a sacrifice most acceptable to God. This character of true repentance is clearly set forth in the Psalms of David; when a person's heart is inwardly torn with grief and weighed down by sorrow and then healed by faith and set free from sin, it is lifted up by divine joy, provoked to good works, and thoroughly transformed and changed. Such a transformation of mind cannot help but lead to an external reformation of life and behaviour.

On the other hand, whoever, out of fear of punishment, avoids openly sinning or devotes themselves to doing good works or bodily penances, but remains unreformed and unregenerate in their heart, not entering into a new and inward life of repentance will, despite the whole train of his external acts, prove at last to be a castaway (1 Cor 9:27). It will not help him to cry "Lord, Lord!" He will hear the terrible declaration, "I never knew you!" (Mat 7:21-23). For it is certain that "not everyone who says "Lord, Lord" will enter the kingdom of heaven, but only those who do the will of their heavenly Father" (Mat 7:21-23). Under this divine judgment, all people are included, regardless of their rank or status, if they do not truly repent and are not new creatures in Christ. As it is written, "If anyone have not the Spirit of Christ, he is none of His" (Rom 8:9).

It is therefore reasonable to assert that those who live a life devoid of repentance, marked by self-interest, pride, selfishness, impatience, envy, self-justification etc., live in the devil and partake of his nature. Despite outward appearances of honesty, covering themselves with a cloak of morality and good behaviour, they are, nevertheless, according to Christ's words to the Jews (John 8:44), inwardly devils. This statement may be uncomfortable, but it is confirmed by Scripture and human experience.

Chapter 5: Righteousness by Faith

Whosoever believeth that Jesus is the Christ, is born of God. - 1 Joh 5:1.

True, or "saving" faith is greatly misunderstood. It is not a self-interested mental assent to religious teachings. It is also more than just having trust, hope, and confidence in God. It is an unwavering dependence on God and His grace through Jesus Christ. It is the same kind of dependence that little children have on their parents and without which no one will "enter into the kingdom of heaven" (Matt 18:3). It is the kind of dependence that Jesus had on his Father when He said, "Verily, verily, I say unto you, The Son can do nothing of himself, but what he seeth the Father do: for what things soever he doeth, these also doeth the Son likewise." (John 5:19, also John 10:14; 12:49-50). Just as there can be no true repentance while there remains any trust, hope or confidence in oneself: one's works, one's will, or one's beliefs, neither can there be any true faith. Since the foundation of repentance is a complete turning away from ourselves unto God, faith is most certainly not trusting in one's own belief about God. True faith is inseparable from true repentance and cannot exist without it. The strength of one's faith is inextricably linked to the depth of one's repentance.

True faith, like repentance, is unnatural to the human heart. It is a gift from God (Rom 12:3), germinating from the seed of His Word, (Luke 8:11) being watered by the Holy Spirit. Those who desire a saving faith in Christ as the Saviour of the world must first have knowledge of Him as revealed in His word as the great example of life. To truly know Christ, they must love and admire the virtues that characterized Him with all their soul, and desire to cultivate them within themselves. They must know Him to be blameless, pure meek, gentle, and loving, composed entirely of patience and humility. They must realise that the Lord has left for them this living example of goodness and piety, for them to carry in their hearts and strive to be transformed into its likeness.

Faith is born as by God's grace the eyes of man are opened and he sees himself as he really is: a slave to selfishness, self-justification, impatience, self-centeredness and pride and realises that, notwithstanding his desires and efforts for goodness, his good motives, good works, moralism, or even belief in God, he cannot escape his inward corruption. His fig leaf of outward righteousness, which he hopes will mitigate his inward corruption, is stripped away, revealing the reality of his self-deception. Seeing no other hope for his soul but Jesus, he cries out, in deep repentance to God as his only hope to be saved from himself.

Together with the apostle Paul he laments "For sin... deceived me... For I delight in the law of God after the inward man, but I see another law in my members, warring against the law of my mind, and bringing me into captivity to the law of sin, which is in my members. O wretched man that I am! Who shall deliver me from the body of this death?" (Rom 7:11, 22-25). The more we realize the utter hopelessness of our spiritual condition and our inability to overcome it, and the more earnestly we reach out to God in desperation for Him to save us from ourselves, the greater our faith becomes. Faith is the act of surrendering ourselves to God, seeking rest in Him alone from the inward strife of self, and the outward trials of life. As confidence in oneself fades (Phil 3:3), faith, being dependence on God, grows.

True faith is not a passive expectation in God but an active dependence on Him. The apostle Paul calls faith a 'substance'; meaning that it is a tangible expression of our dependence on God for "things hoped for". A passive expectation is not tangible, but diligently seeking and pleading with God is (Heb 11:6). Faith is a tangible agent for making things that do not exist become real by creating a conduit for God's promises to be fulfilled. It is a catalyst bringing tangible reality to the intangible, giving substance to the otherwise invisible. The less our immediate dependence, on and seeking for God, the smaller the conduit of faith becomes. When it has devolved into just a passive expectation based on feelings, religious belief or some past experience, it ceases to be faith and becomes presumption. At that point, faith is dead and one's hope is vain, trust is misplaced, and confidence is foolishness.

The idea of an 'active' faith is commonly misunderstood to mean having religious convictions that demand outward actions; charity, devotion and/or obedience to the law. These works, however, do not constitute any part of faith, nor are they necessarily the fruit of faith. In many instances, they are just the sincere result of moralism or Pharisaism. Faith does not depend on the will or efforts of man to bear fruit of righteousness in the life but solely depends on God's will and power. Accordingly, the work of faith (Gal 5:6) is not primarily in external actions, but rather an inner seeking and pleading with God, and this is where our efforts must be placed. The resulting fruits – practical expressions of love and service towards God and our neighbours, contribute nothing to faith, but rather are a testimony to the power of God to transform the heart and life of those who have such a faith.

Faith is rooted in the unfailing mercy and merits of Christ alone for salvation. Not only do external works contribute nothing to faith, but also they contribute nothing to our being accepted of God (Rom 3:20; Gal 2:16). The Bible warns us against being "unequally yoked" (2 Cor 6:14), meaning that we should not mix our faith in Jesus with any dependence on our own works, belief, or feeling, as this would create a shaky and unstable foundation, resulting in an ungrounded hope built on divided trust and confidence. True faith can only exist when all self-reliance and self-confidence is abandoned. Our faith then rests on a firm and solid foundation, and remains unmoved by perplexity and doubts. The assurance of faith is not in our own belief in Christ, but that if we depend on Him, He will never fail us. All righteousness in man's life proceeds from Christ alone through faith, not from the beliefs, works or will of man, and without that righteousness, no man shall enter the kingdom of God. This righteousness is twofold: imputed and imparted, also known as justification and sanctification. By justification, one receives forgiveness for sins and is accepted of God and by sanctification, one is enabled to do works of righteousness. Both are the result of the new birth that occurs when faith and repentance are created in the soul through the agency of the Holy Spirit.

As a dead man cannot do anything unless he is first raised from the dead and given a new principle of life, so too, the principles of faith and repentance are the basis for spiritual life, by which a man who is dead in trespasses and sins, is raised unto righteousness by Jesus Christ. By birth, we inherit the roots of Adam's carnal nature that germinated from the serpent's seed that was planted in him at his fall. By faith we are cut away from Adam's roots of self-centeredness and pride and grafted into Christ, the living and blessed vine (John 15:4). Just as a scion is grafted onto a good root for no other end than that it may bear fruit, and is nourished by the sap of the root which causes it to grow, flourish, and bear fruit, so too when, through faith in Christ, His Spirit flows within us, we grow in the spirit and bear the fruit of righteousness. As the fruit from a grafted tree can never replace the tree which bears it, this righteousness can, however, never replace nor reduce our need of ongoing faith and repentance.

If having obtained righteousness by faith, whether imputed or imparted, we rest our hope, trust or confidence on that righteousness, then we cease to have faith. We become like the complacent Pharisee in the parable, who placed his confidence on the righteousness he believed he had obtained from God rather than on God's mercy alone and as a result was not heard of God (Luk 18:10-14; Phil 3:12). There is no point in the Christian life where we need less of God's continued mercy and help than does the disbelieving open sinner. Our dependence on God is not lessened because we believe in His word, have accepted His grace and no longer live in open defiance of His law. If anything, these things lead to an increased realisation of our dependence on Christ. Having obtained the gift of righteousness (Rom 5:17) it must be maintained by faith (Heb 3:14) as Jesus said "Watch and pray, that ye enter not into temptation: the spirit indeed is willing, but the flesh is weak" (Matt 26:41) and all the righteousness we have to our account will not be counted in the day that we sin wilfully by turning away from God and depend on ourselves (Heb 10:26-27 ; 2 Pet 2:20-21; Eze 18:24).

Furthermore the evidence of living faith, as noted earlier is not in anything that makes one "appear outwardly righteous before men" (Mat 23:28) whether it be profession of faith, works of charity, devotion, or keeping of the law. The Pharisees did all these things (Luke 11:39-44, 20:46-47; Mat 6:1-7; 23:5-6, 15, 23) but had no real faith nor repentance (Luke 13:3). When Jesus declared "ye shall know them by their fruits" (Mat 7:16), He did not mean that that the cleanness of the outside of the cup, nor the whiteness of their sepulchres (Mat 23:26-28), are evidence of true faith, but rather "fruit meet for" or befitting repentance (Luke 3:8; Acts 26:20). This fruit of repentance tends to brokenness rather than self-satisfaction, self-abasement (before God rather than men) rather than self-promotion, selflessness rather than self-interest, and entire dependence on God rather than self-assurance, self-reliance or self-confidence.

A good barometer of faith is secret prayer, which is the outcry of a self-abasing, contrite heart. Those with the greatest need of, and dependence on God, and consequently the greatest faith, pray most frequently. No matter how eloquent, graceful or sincere a prayer may appear to the uncircumcised in heart, prayers that rather than being contrite, focus mostly on praise, gratitude or selfish wants like that of the self-assured Pharisee in the parable or those that are formal, scripted or mindlessly repetitive are indicative of a dead faith.

How can anyone expect to be accepted of God, forgiven and set free from sin when they are at peace with their carnal spirit and its sinfulness? Surely, nothing could be more preposterous or absurd than to expect that their selfishness, pride and secret sins would be pardoned if they are still rejoicing in them with no intention to renounce them. It is equally nonsensical to seek comfort in Christ's suffering and death, yet continue to wallow in self-love, self-will, self-honour, self-interest, and self-confidence, which are the cause of Christ's death. Despite the obvious truth that repentance is necessary for forgiveness, many people claim to be Christians while continuing to indulge in the anger, selfishness, pride, malice, envy, unrighteousness and self-righteousness of the flesh. They expect forgiveness, and presume to apply the merits of Christ as a defence against God's judgment, without changing their ways. This is a gross error, but they try to justify it by calling it faith. They flatter and deceive themselves to their own destruction; fondly supposing that they are true Christians because they mentally assent to the Gospel, and believe that Jesus died for their sins. However, this is not faith, but mere fantasy. The Bible clearly teaches that to be a true Christian, one must not only accept the teachings of the Gospel, but also have genuine repentance, turning away from one's carnal spirit and living a life fully surrendered to Him.

The man whose entire dependence is upon Christ has a bond with Him so close and strong that neither life nor death can break it (Rom. 8:38; 2 Tim. 1:12). He cannot bear to live without Christ, and would gladly rather die than live apart from Christ. Such a faith must be kindled in our soul by the Holy Spirit who infuses heavenly strength in us that empowers us to overcome the fear of death and the love of the world. This is why "whatsoever is born of God overcometh the world." All the promises and power of an omnipotent God are at hand to those who vigorously depend on God and God alone to overcome the world. "With men this is impossible; but with God all things are possible" (Mat19:26). Our faith is the victory that overcomes the world (1 John 5:4). Faith binds us to God, and is the key that unlocks all of heaven's treasures, enabling us to partake of all things that are of God and Christ and makes us one with Him. Faith makes us sons of God, and joint-heirs with the Lord Jesus Christ. Wherever true faith exists, Christ is truly present with all His merits, grace, and freedom from sin. From Him we ask and receive pardon, divine power and strength to overcome, increased faith and repentance. The vigour of our faith is the foundation of inner strength, the might of the spirit, the source of holy boldness, confidence, and our assurance toward God (2 Tim. 2:1; Eph. 3:12, 16; Phil. 1:14; 1 John 3:21; 1 Thess. 1:5; 2:2).

Faith at first is like a newborn child, clothed in the mercy of God but weak, helpless and hungering, thirsting and crying out after righteousness. It receives all from God and, partaking of His goodness, grows from day to day and as it grows so also does grace, strength, truth, love, mercy, humility, meekness, chastity, righteousness, wisdom, understanding, spiritual discernment and holiness. It brings peace, joy, patience, and comfort in adversity. Through faith the whole kingdom of God descends into man, it overcomes the world and renews the whole man, purifies the heart, sanctifies the soul and delivers him from the corruption that is within himself.

The consolation of such a faith is so powerful that it convinces the heart of divine truth by inward experience and by tasting the heavenly goodness in the soul and the peace of God, which passes all understanding. If someone does not experience the joy and consoling influence of faith, they should not despair. They should not trust their own feelings, but instead, they should trust in the mercy and love of God, which remains sure and eternal. Even if we stumble and fall due to our human weaknesses, we can return to God by genuine repentance and more carefully watching against sin. The grace of God will not be withdrawn if we seek it with sincerity. For Christ is and will ever be *Christ* and a Saviour, whether the faith that embraces Him be strong or weak. His grace is always sufficient for us, and His strength is made perfect in our weakness. If we wait patiently for Him, and hold onto our faith, the Lord will visit our souls in His own time with a sense of His gracious favour and abundant consolations, even if we do not feel it at present (Heb 10:36).

Chapter 6. Living by Every Word of God

Man shall not live by bread alone, but by every word that proceedeth out of the mouth of God. – Matt 4:4

Man's wellbeing depends on his regeneration and renewal, and God ordained that the changes that must take place spiritually within us by faith should be outwardly revealed in the words of Scripture. Therefore, we must learn for ourselves what it is that the Scripture reveals and embrace it by faith. The Word is like a seed planted within us (Luke 8:11), and it must grow and produce fruit. If we fail to experience this spiritual transformation, the Word is to us a dead seed, lifeless and ineffective.

To illustrate this consider the case of Cain and Abel. They represent the behaviour and actions of the old and the new man in the heart of the believer. Abel was happy to surrender his will and comply with all of God's requirements. Cain also believed in God but refused to surrender all of His will, and only obeyed God as it pleased himself, without repentance. If, like Cain, our belief in God leads to sacrificial works, but only to the extent that we desire, rather than fully surrendering to His will, as revealed in His every word, then our faith is not in God but in ourselves, because we depend on our own judgement rather than His. Cain perpetually tried to destroy Abel, which represents the daily strife of the flesh and spirit, and the enmity subsisting between the seed of the serpent and the seed of the woman.

In the case of Abraham, we learn that the Christian is required to surrender his own life and desires to God, even all that he possesses, in order that he may walk before God with a perfect heart, obtain the victory, and enter into the land of promise and kingdom of heaven. Such is the meaning of the Lord's words: "If any man come to me, and hate not his father, and mother, and wife, and children, and brethren, and sisters, yea, and his own life also, he cannot be my disciple;" that is, he must renounce all these rather than renounce Christ (Luke 14:26). Lot, symbolizes our need to forsake the world and its wicked ways and obey God's commands, not looking back with Lot's wife (Luke 17:32), in order to be saved. Whatever is recorded of the Mosaic priesthood, the tabernacle, the Ark of the Covenant, or the mercy seat, with the sacrifices, the Day of Atonement with its affliction of soul etc., – all have relation to the Christian believer. The believer must pray in spirit and in truth; burn spiritual incense; and slay the sin offering by presenting his body, through mortification of his mind and spirit, as a reasonable service and sacrifice, so that Christ may truly dwell in him by faith.

When we look to the New Testament, we also see an outward expression of truths that are to be inwardly experienced by faith. When we become a new creation in Christ, it is essential that we live and walk in harmony with Him, fleeing from worldly ambitions and desires and living as strangers on earth. We should emulate His virtues, such as humility, contempt for the world, meekness, and patience, and strive to demonstrate love, longsuffering, and charity towards others. In and through Christ we should exercise mercy, a forgiving spirit, and love towards our enemies, and together with Him, do the Father's will. We must also face temptation with Christ and, with Him, overcome it. We may be ridiculed, despised, and persecuted for our faith, just as Christ was. If necessary, we should be willing to die for the truth that is within us, and, if necessary, we should die for and with Him just as the martyrs did before us, as a testament that He, by faith, lives in us and we in Him.

This is what it means to be conformed to the image of Christ; to be born anew in Christ; to put on Christ. To grow into Christ and be strong in Him. To live with Christ in exile; to be baptised into His baptism; to be mocked and crucified like Him; to die with Him; to be buried with Him and to rise from the dead with Him and to reign with Him for all eternity. If we truly desire to be united with Christ as our Head and Saviour, we must in this way die daily with Him and crucify the flesh (Rom 6:5-6). If we do not choose this path, Christ will not be in us but remain outside of us, far away from our faith, heart, and mind, and be of no benefit to us. But if we allow Him to dwell in our hearts through faith, He will be our strength, comfort, and salvation.

This is the effect of faith: the Word of God comes alive in our hearts, as it were a living embodiment in us of those things that it externally declares. This is why faith is referred to as a substance and evidence (Heb 11:1), as it brings the Scriptures to life within us. As a result, every sermon, discourse, and epistle contained in the Word of God; whether spoken by Christ, written by the prophets or the apostles – as they relate to their complete fulfilment – are clearly intended to be fulfilled within each individual. It is not just the plain doctrines that belong to us, but also the parables and miracles that abound in the life of Christ. All these have their ultimate spiritual fulfilment in our own experience. When we read about Christ healing others, we learn how we must come to Christ in order to be healed from our spiritual ailment. Recognising that nothing in this world but Christ is our only hope, we must earnestly seek Him until we have found Him, humbly willing to do whatever He requires of us. When we read about Him curing the blind, we can believe that He will restore spiritual sight to us who by nature are spiritually blind. Similarly, we can apply every one of Christ's miracles to our own lives. Only realise that you are spiritually blind, lame, deaf, or a leper – dead in trespasses and sins – then Christ can heal your soul and bring to life that which is dead and so take part in the first resurrection.

When Jesus declared, "man shall not live by bread alone but by every word that proceeds out of the mouth of God," (Mat 4:4) He was not only talking about learning spiritual lessons from the events described in the Bible. He was specifically talking about obeying and trusting the entirety of God's word, even as He gave us an example of doing so. This includes obeying not just the commands of Jesus but also the law of God. It is not that man spiritually lives by obeying the law, but that not doing so is evidence that he is spiritually dead. The law cannot give life, it can only bring death (Rom 8:2; 1 Cor 15:56; 2 Cor 3:6). No one lives by moving, but if they do not move, it is because they are dead. Also while a dead body can be made to move that does not prove that it is alive. The meticulous keeping of the law by the spiritually dead scribes and Pharisees in Jesus' day demonstrate that the keeping of the law neither engenders spiritual life nor is any evidence of it. Neither of these is the purpose of the law, rather it is to reveal to us our depravity and sinfulness, to bring us to repentance and to drive us to Christ (Gal 3:24; Rom 3:20, 10:4). This is the only role of the law in the process by which spiritual life is born and maintained. To set aside the law is to set aside our need of Christ.

The law of God, as expressed in His word, is but a clarification and expansion of the natural law that God has put into every one that is born into this world (Rom 2:15), by which they distinguish between good and evil; honour and shame. In addition to natural law, God's Word and their conscience, Christians who claim to be under the new covenant make themselves accountable to a fourth testimony against themselves. This is the new covenant of which God says, "I will put my law in their inward parts, and... in their hearts... for they shall all know me, from the least of them unto the greatest of them, saith the Lord" (Jer. 31:33, 34; John 6:45). If God abandoned the heathen to their own blindness and depraved minds because they were disobedient to this natural law; or as the apostle Paul expresses it, "because they did not like to retain God in their knowledge," (Rom. 1:28); how much more will those who have received the Word of God, yet disregard it, be condemned to eternal damnation?

The apostle warns us about the consequences of ignoring or deliberately disobeying God. He does not mean rejecting the Gospel as a whole, or ignoring the claims of the law entirely, but choosing to selectively neglect parts of God's word. "If," says the apostle, "we sin wilfully, after that we have received the knowledge of the truth, there remaineth no more sacrifice for sins, but a certain fearful looking for of judgment and fiery indignation, which shall devour the adversaries. He that despised Moses' law," continues the Apostle, "died without mercy under two or three witnesses; of how much sorer punishment, suppose ye, shall he be thought worthy, who hath trodden underfoot the Son of God, and hath counted the blood of the covenant, wherewith he was sanctified, an unholy thing, and hath done despite unto the spirit of grace? For we know him that hath said, Vengeance belongeth unto me, I will recompense, saith the Lord. It is a fearful thing to fall into the hands of the living God." (Heb. 10:26-31). These words are not meant for those who stumble through weakness, but for those who deliberately sin against their knowledge and continue to live in this state of stubbornness until the end. If faith is depending only on God and His every word, then we have no faith if we depend on ourselves or others to decide which portions of God's Words are applicable and which are not (Jer 17:5).

In summary, the Scriptures bear an outward testimony to those things that are to be inwardly fulfilled in man by faith. It reveals the external image that is to be formed internally. It describes the kingdom of God in the letter, which is to be established in the heart, after the spirit. It reveals Christ outwardly who is to live within me. All of this is to be accomplished by faith or scripture will be of no profit whatsoever. This is what it means when it says to live "by every word that proceedeth out of the mouth of God" (Mat 4:4).

Chapter 7. Blessed are they that Mourn

To this man will I look, even to him that is poor and of a contrite spirit, and trembleth at my word.—Isaiah 66:2.

These comforting words are spoken by our gracious and merciful God, through the prophet, to lift up those whose hearts are filled with misery and sorrow. So do not be ashamed of being bruised in spirit and abased in your own eyes. Humble yourself in the dust, and consider yourself unworthy of all grace and favour; and so doing you will be raised out of your degradation and be accepted through Christ by Almighty God. Those who do not give up all sense of their own goodness or self-worth are not truly humble or broken-hearted and have no right to expect God's favour. "If anyone thinks he is something when he is nothing, he deceives himself." (Gal 6:3). The reason is that God is all in all, alone, and in comparison every other creature is seemingly insignificant: a mere nothing. So great and so practical is this truth that man is not only to believe it in his heart, but also to express it in his life and conduct.

If it is your intention to give God all glory and honour, then you must first become nothing in your own eyes; and have a very low opinion of yourself, and of your spiritual advancement. For, how is it possible for God to be all in all while you continue to be something? When you exalt yourself, you are actually usurping God's sovereignty and claiming for yourself what belongs to Him alone. By doing so, you are stealing the glory that rightfully belongs to God. Consider David's words to his wife Michal, who criticized him: "It was before the Lord," he said, "and I will yet be more vile than thus, and will be base in mine own sight." (2 Sam 6:21-22). In other words, David was willing to abase and humble himself before God, acknowledging that He is the only one who deserves glory and honour.

A person who wants to be something is the material God makes into nothing. But someone who loves to be reputed as nothing and who in their own judgement is so, is the raw material that God uses to make something extraordinary. Those who are wise in their own eyes are the ones God turns into fools, while those who acknowledge their own foolishness and nothingness are the ones God transforms into wise and great individuals.

True Christianity

Those who think they are spiritually rich will be exposed as "wretched, and miserable, and poor, and blind, and naked" (Rev 3:17), while those who are poor in spirit will inherit the kingdom of heaven. The person who before the Lord sincerely confesses that he is the most unworthy and miserable of all men, is, in the sight of God, the greatest of all men. He who believes himself to be the chief of sinners, shall be honoured by the Lord as the chief of saints (Mat 23:12, Luke 1:52).

This is the humility that God exalts; that misery that He values; that nothing from which He creates something. Just as at creation, the glorious frame of heaven and earth was made out of nothing, so too, must man be reduced to a profound sense of his own degradation and nothingness if he is ever to be lifted up to glory and dignity. Take David, for example. God saw his misery and granted him the richest gifts of his grace. Or Jacob who confessed, "I am not worthy of the least of all thy mercies." (Gen. 32:10). Above all, consider the example of Christ, the ultimate model of what it means to be a Christian. He was brought below the lowest of men, to that of a worm and a curse for our sake (Psa 22:6). He was despised and rejected of men (Isa 53:3) but the lower He sunk, the higher he arose afterwards, and received a name that is above every name.

But who is that humble and selfless individual who sees themselves as nothing in their own eyes? It is the person who, deep down, knows they are unworthy of any divine favour, whether physical or spiritual. Anyone who thinks they are deserving of something, because they think they are something, are really the farthest away from divine grace and the new creation. The spirit of self is so destructive that it makes grace of no effect and shuts out all of its blessings. If we think we deserve something, then it is not God's gift to us. In reality, whatever we are, is because of God's grace, not our own goodness or efforts. We cannot call anything our own except our sins, helplessness, and misery. The rest belongs to God.

Independent from God, by whom he subsists, man is like a shadow. As a shadow of a tree constantly follows the shape of the tree that casts it, so we should follow God's will. As the Bible says, "In him we live, and move, and have our being" (Acts 17:28). While the fruit of the tree may sometimes appear in the shadow, it does not belong to the shadow but to the tree: so all the good fruits that may appear in your life and conduct, are not the produce of your own self and ability, but of God alone, who is the source of all good fruits. Just as the fruit grows from the tree's inner energy, activated from above not from the visible bark, so the new man and the fruit he bears, does not spring up from what is physical or visible to the eye, but from a supernatural and invisible seed. Now, man is by nature a dry tree; but God is his strength, who revives, nourishes, and makes him flourish in the house of God. God is the "strength of our life" (Psa. 27:1), says the Psalmist: and so we "shall bring forth much fruit whilst we abide in Christ." (John 15:5).

We should not interpret 'the poor and contrite man,' as someone who is only poor outwardly in terms of material possessions or human help and relief. Instead, it is a person who is burdened by their spiritual poverty and sins and grieves over them. When a man is wretched and poor in his own eyes, and has nothing to cling to but the pure grace of God, revealed in Christ Jesus, then God "looks upon him" graciously. This divine regard is not a mere human gaze, destitute of life and virtue, but is accompanied with a living power and influence that supports and revives the faint and penitent sinner. None but the self-abasing and contrite are capable of this heavenly regard, and as they receive this consolation from God, they are more aware of their unworthiness. Recognising that God's grace is not something that can be earned, such a man deems that he is undeserving of any blessing, whether divine or temporal, only deserving God's wrath and eternal damnation. He says with Jacob, "I am not worthy of the least of all the mercies, and of all the truth which you hast shewed unto thy servant:" for since thou gave me thy Son Jesus Christ, I come with two blessings; thy grace and thy glory. (Gen. 32:10). Even if one were to cry a sea of tears, it would not be enough to earn or deserve the slightest measure of heavenly blessing.

Whoever in this way realises by faith his own misery, is truly one of those poor and contrite men on whom the Lord graciously looks. Without this brokenness of heart, man cannot expect to enjoy the blessings of God, nor that grace and mercy which is promised to the poor in spirit only. In this weakness and poverty, the apostle glories when he says, "If I must needs glory, I will glory of the things which concern mine infirmities" (2 Cor. 11:30): and he adds the reason, "that the power of Christ may rest upon me" (2 Cor. 12:9). For so great is God's mercy, that He will not allow the work of His hands to be destroyed: but the weaker the creature is in itself, the more is it sustained by the power of the Almighty. For in the weakness of the creature the power of God is exalted, as the Lord declared unto Paul: "My grace is sufficient for thee; for my strength is made perfect in weakness." (v.9). The more degraded and miserable a Christian is in his own opinion, the more favourably God looks upon him, and the more abundantly shares with him the riches of His glory. In granting this heavenly consolation, which infinitely surpasses any human comfort, God does not look at man's goodness or works in the least, but only on his want and poverty. God sees the contrite and comforts his spirit.

What does man have left to boast about or what can he say when he speaks up? The best course is to simply say, 'Lord, Have mercy on me!' And truly, God does not require anything more than that man genuinely detest his sin and in a genuine expression of repentance pray for forgiveness. Do not cry about your physical struggles, such as hunger, cold, sickness or persecution, or imprisonment. If sin did not exist, there would be no misery. But no matter how much misery we now have, we deserve still more. (Psa.103:10). We should not complain that we do not have many temporal benefits, since we do not deserve even the smallest of them. Our flesh and blood may find this difficult to accept, but every penitent sinner should be a harsh critic of themselves and give no quarter to their own sinful inclinations. This is the path to obtaining God's favour and mercy.

Instead, humble yourself before the Lord and lament your wretched state, trapped in a house of sin and death, which is your flesh. As the apostle Paul said, "O wretched man that I am, who will deliver me from this body of death?" (Rom 7:24). This honest acknowledgment of your own inner misery, this godly sorrow, this thirst for divine grace, and this faith leaning on Christ alone – all these open the door to God's grace in Christ. The Lord says, "Be zealous, therefore, and repent. Behold, I stand, at the door and knock; if any man hear my voice, and open the door, I will come in to him, and sup with him, and he with me" (Rev. 3:20). This is the door of faith (Acts 14:27), through which the Lord enters our souls; refreshing us with the light of His presence after the day of struggle is over. Then it is, that "mercy and truth meet together; righteousness and peace kiss each other; that truth springs out of the earth, and righteousness looks down from heaven." (Ps. 85:10, 11). Then it is that the woman, that poor sinner but now a penitent, anoints the feet of her

Lord, washes them with tears, and wipes them with the hairs of her head, expressing thereby all the marks of an unfeigned and deep humility. (Luke 7:37). Then it is, that the spiritual priest (Rev. 1:6), in the holy ornaments of faith, offers up the true sacrifice, even a broken and lowly spirit, with the incense of true contrition and prayer (Ps. 51:19). Then it is that the true sanctified water of purification (Num. 8:7) is applied,—the tears which grief for sin caused to flow; and now, through faith and by the power of the blood of Christ, the spiritual Israelite is washed and cleansed.

Blessed is the one who feels the weight of their sin in their heart, and even more blessed is the one who responds to this call to repentance by embracing a genuine sorrow for their mistakes. This godly sorrow is a gift from the Holy Spirit, and it arises from reflecting on God's law and the righteousness and sacrifice of Jesus Christ. It reveals both the severity of God's wrath against sin and the depths of His love for the sinner. As Jesus shed His blood to atone for our sins, His love compelled Him to die for us while we were still sinners. Romans 5:8 says that here, God's justice and mercy come together to bring salvation to our souls. And this, Christian, is how you, by realising your own misery together with faith, being unwavering dependence on Christ, can obtain the favour of God. To sum it up, the more wretched and miserable any one is in his own judgment, the more dearly he will be loved of God, and the more graciously will the Lord bestow His favour upon him.

Chapter 8. Love God with All Your Heart

Jesus said unto him, Thou shalt love the Lord thy God with all thy heart, and with all thy soul, and with all thy mind. This is the first and great commandment. – Matt 22:37-38

He that loveth his life shall lose it; and he that hateth his life in this world shall keep it unto life eternal.—John 12:25.

If any man come to me, and hate not ... his own life also, he cannot be my disciple. – Luke 14:26.

It is a fundamental aspect of a faithful wife to please her husband alone. So, are you seeking to please yourself and the world, when you can be united to Christ, the great lover of souls? Let go and sincerely despise all that is in the world, so you can be worthy of the eminent dignity of being spiritually married to Christ. If your love is not solely united to Christ, it is an unfaithful and adulterous love and not the kind that a Christian should have for their Saviour. A Christian's love for Christ must be pure and undivided. The Law of Moses required that the priest marry virgins (Lev. 21:13, 14); and Christ, our High Priest, will unite himself only to a virgin soul; one that is attached to nothing that the world can offer, but solely to himself; one that loves Him more than itself. "If any man come to me," He says, "and hate not his own life, he cannot be my disciple." (Luke 14:26).

To understand what it means to hate ourselves, we must remember that we carry about with us "the old man," and we are indeed the old man himself. His nature is to hurry from one sin to another, to love himself, to pursue his own profit and honour, to be self-sufficient, and to indulge his own will and inclinations. The flesh is always the same: always considering itself, easily wounded, envious, bitter, covetous, and looking for revenge. This is the very essence of your life, of the old man within you from which all these sinful compulsions proceed. If you want to be a disciple of Christ you must, of necessity hate yourself and your own natural life. Whoever loves himself, must also love his own pride and avarice, his own anger, impatience and hatred, envy and lying, dishonesty and sinfulness; and, in short, he must love all the fruit of unholy desires and a corrupt heart. But if you really want to be a Christian, you must not love, nor excuse, nor lessen your sins, but must hate them, forsake them, and subdue them, engaging in a continual war against your corrupt spirit and the flesh.

Self-love is the greatest obstacle to humanity's eternal salvation. This is not referring to the natural love that motivates self-preservation. Rather, it is about the carnal and unwarranted regard that makes us solely concerned about ourselves, without reference to the great Author of Life. Man was created to love God alone, and since God only is to be loved, anyone who loves themselves is an idolater, making themselves their own god. Our hearts find joy and rest in the object of our affection and, whatever that may be, we become bound to it and devoted to it. As a result, we become slaves to our desires and are deprived of that true freedom with which man was originally created. In this fallen state, we are forced to serve multiple masters, as many as there are objects of our affection. But if we truly fix our love on God, we are free to serve only Him, and we preserve our liberty with all its privileges.

Therefore, it is crucial to be mindful of our life and conduct, lest we hinder the progress of divine love in our soul. If we want to experience God alone, we must surrender ourselves fully to Him. If we love and please ourselves instead of loving and pleasing God, we will inevitably face sorrow, fear, and anxiety. On the other hand, if we yield ourselves entirely to God, clinging to and delighting in Him alone, He will never leave us nor forsake us. He will remove all fear and anxiety from our minds. However, those who pursue their own interests in every situation and who are constantly seeking profit, praise and their own desires can never obtain true peace of mind. There will always be something that disrupts their desires and disturbs their rest.

The things we value in life – praise, wealth, and pleasure – are fleeting and perishable, tied to a world that is also transient. In contrast, the love of God endures forever. Accordingly, any sense of satisfaction or peace that is built on loving ourselves and earthly things cannot last, it would be disrupted by every minor setback or change that comes our way. But when our minds are fixed on God and His love, we cannot help but remain in a state of perfect peace and calm, no matter what life throws our way. Do not be fooled into thinking that fame, wealth, or honour will always bring you good fortune. In fact, a righteous rejection of these transient things – even an elimination of our love for them – would bring infinite blessings and advantages. So, let go of everything, and through faith, you will regain it all again and more. You will never find the true God if you love yourself and the world.

Unwarranted self-love is rooted in the world, not in God: it is earthly. It is the main obstacle to "the wisdom that comes from above" (Jam 3:17) which does not crave human approval or praise. While it is "a pearl of great price," (Matt. 13:46), it goes unnoticed and unappreciated in the world. While some may claim to possess this wisdom, it remains hidden from those who do not apply it in practice in their daily lives. If you want to experience this wisdom, let go of all that human wisdom which "puffeth up" (1 Cor. 8:1), together with your pride and self-love. Trade in your earthly wisdom, which is admired by the world, for the heavenly and divine wisdom that comes from God. Then, instead of the wisdom of this world which is characterised by self-importance and the approval of others, you will obtain a wisdom that is overlooked and rejected by the world but is of divine origin and eternal duration.

It is impossible to love God until you abhor yourself; that is, until you are disgusted with yourself and your sinfulness, until you crucify your carnal nature along with its sinful inclinations and your self-will. The more you strive to love God, the more effort you will make to overcome your own selfish desires and carnal instincts. The more you surrender and abandon yourself and self-love by the power of the Spirit of God, the closer you will come, through faith, to God and His divine love. Since inner peace depends on being free from worldly desires, when you break free from the things that bind you to the creature and return to God alone, you will find rest.

David practised the duty of self-abandonment when he forsook his palace in Jerusalem and was reviled by Shimei, for he said, "The Lord hath said unto him, Curse David." (2 Sam. 16:10). As if he had said: "I am a worm in the sight of God, and deserve to suffer far worse things." And this is how all the holy men of old and prophets of God freely denied their own will, and counted themselves unworthy of every blessing. They endured their trials with patience (Acts 5:40, 41); they did not retaliate when cursed; they blessed their persecutors, and prayed for their murderers (Acts 7:60); and so, "through much tribulation, entered into the kingdom of God." (Acts 14:22). This pattern of self-abandonment is seen in those who acknowledge their own unworthiness of any favour or blessing and believe that they deserve all the evils that can come their way.

Now, this self-abandonment or self-denial is the cross of Christ, which He has called us to bear, saying, "If any man will come after me, let him deny himself and take up his cross daily, and follow me." (Luke 9:23). This self-denying life is a severe cross to the flesh; the natural man desires a life free from restraint and contradiction, and would follow the inclination of his own will, and seek his own ease and pleasure, rather than the humility, patience, and meekness of Christ, with the other graces that characterise His life and example.

Those who genuinely want to deny themselves must follow not their own will but the will of Christ who declared, "I am the way, and the truth, and the life." (John 14:6). As if He had said, "Without a way, no man walks; without the truth, nothing is known; and without life, no man lives. So, look to me as the way that you must walk, the truth you must believe, and the life you must live. I am the unerring way, the infallible truth, and the eternal life. The way to eternal life is through my merit; the truth itself is in my word; and life is possible through the power of my resurrection. So, if you continue in the way, the truth will guide you to eternal life. If you want to stay on track, follow me; if you want to know the truth, believe in me; and if you want to experience life everlasting, put your complete trust in me, who for your sake endured the death of the cross."

What way, truth, and life surpasses all others? Surely there is no way but through the holy and precious merits of Christ; no truth, but His eternal Word; and no life, but life eternal. If you want to be raised up with Christ Jesus into heaven, believe in Him here and follow His example of humility. This is the safe way to eternal glory. If you want to escape the world's temptations, take hold of His word by faith and follow the example He has left for us to imitate; because that is the infallible truth. And if you want to live with Christ, then die with Him and in Him unto sin, and become a new creation; for this is life. In this way, Christ is the way, the truth, and the life – both by his example and in His merit.

"Be ye followers of God as dear children." Eph. 5:1.

Let us focus on living a life that resembles Christ's life. If we did not have anything else to distinguish true Christians from false ones, Christ's example alone would be enough. When we consider that Christ, our Lord, spent His life in pain and suffering, we should be ashamed to spend our lives in ease and comfort. If a soldier forgets his own comfort when he sees his captain fighting for his life, why do we pursue worldly pleasures and honours when our Prince was treated with such shame and sacrificed Himself on the cross for us? Doesn't that mean we're not truly fighting under His banner?

Many people today want to be considered Christians, but how many imitate the life and manner of Christ? If being a follower of Christ meant striving for honours and possessions, our Lord would never have taught that these things are worthless compared to heavenly treasures. Look at Christ's life and teachings, and you will see that nothing could be more at odds with the world. Think about the manger and the stable – do not they show a contempt for worldly things? And will Christ's example lead us astray? No! He is the way, the truth, and His life, as understood through His teachings, is the only way to keep us from making mistakes and guard us from the world's delusions and errors.

Christ chose to enter His glory through suffering and shame, why do you insist on making your way to hell through worldly display and vanities? Come back, then, O misguided soul! Escape from the broad path that leads to death and the enjoyment of "the pleasures of sin for a season" (Heb. 11:25). Instead, enter this safe path where you will not go astray; embrace this truth that can never deceive; and live in Him who is Life itself. This way is the truth, and this truth is the way. How blind we are! A worm of the earth would make itself great in the world, while the Lord of glory humbled Himself to the dust. O faithful soul! When your bridegroom comes to meet you, clothed in humility, come down from your pride and ambition, and descend into the valley of humility to meet him, and he will receive you with joy. Just as Abraham left his father's house to go to a land that the Lord was to show him (Gen 12:1). As a true child of Abraham, you must leave behind the pleasure house of self-will and self-love in order to obtain the divine blessing.

When self-professed Christians continue to live for themselves, they are essentially crucifying Christ all over again, making a mockery of His sacrifice. They are profaning the blood of the covenant, despising the Holy Spirit and resisting His work, and by doing so, they are rejecting the grace of God offered through Jesus Christ. As a result, the blood of the Saviour cries out for vengeance against them, and God's righteous judgment will surely fall upon them. This is a terrifying thought that should strike fear into every person who claims to be a Christian. Indeed, it is a sobering reality to consider falling into the hands of a living God, who is capable of punishing those who scorn His grace and mercy.

Self-love distorts our judgment, obscures our understanding, and clouds our reasoning. It seduces the will, corrupts the conscience, closes the gates of life and acknowledges neither God nor neighbour. It is a destructive force that prioritizes earthly pursuits over eternal life. It banishes virtue; seeks after honours, riches, and pleasures; and, in a word, prefers earth to heaven. He, therefore, who thus "loveth his life, shall lose it; but he that hateth his life" (that is, resists this principle of self-love), "shall keep it unto life eternal." (Joh 12:25). Self-love and self-honour prevent us from repenting and is the cause of damnation. Those who are controlled by these are unable to recognize their own degradation and the true nature of sin. They are destitute of humility and are blind to their sin. As a result; they never can obtain pardon or freedom from sin, though they cry out for it with tears; their tears not being shed because they have offended God, but merely on account of the personal loss which they expect to sustain. Self-love is the root of stubbornness and the cause of eternal separation from God.

"The kingdom of heaven is compared in Scripture to "a pearl of great price" which to obtain a man sold all that he had (Mat 13:45-46). This pearl is God Himself, and the eternal life that He has promised, which we can only obtain by giving up everything else including ourselves. We see this same sacrifice in Jesus Christ, who loved not Himself, but left heaven, gave up everything and emptied Himself for our benefit (Eph 5:2; Luke 19:10). Will you hesitate to empty yourself and with all your heart, love Him who gave up everything for you?

Chapter 9. Pilgrims and Strangers

We brought nothing into this world, and it is certain we can carry nothing out. And having food and raiment, let us be therewith content.—1 Tim. 6:7, 8.

Christ, says the apostle, "died for all, that they which live should not henceforth live unto themselves, but unto him which died for them, and rose again." (2 Cor. 5:15) This statement is not only a source of divine comfort, telling us that Jesus died for everyone, but it also teaches a vital lesson: we should not live for ourselves but for Him who died for us. However, it is impossible to live for Him until we are dead to ourselves. If you want to truly live for Christ, you must be willing to die to the world and to yourself. But if you are inclined to live to the world and yourself, it is clear that you must renounce your connection with the Saviour. For "what communion hath light with darkness," Christ with the world, or the Spirit with the flesh (2 Cor 6:14-15).

When the flesh is honoured, wooed, praised, and is surrounded by the luxuries and pleasures of this life it is highly gratified. However, the yoke of Christ requires us to sacrifice our desires for honour, wealth, and recognition, choosing instead to endure shame, contempt, and poverty. We must account ourselves unworthy of these things and freely give up all that the world greatly esteems. This is where the humility and life of Christ are most evident. This is the yoke and the burden we are called to carry, one that is easy and light to the spirit. It is the law of love, whose commands are not grievous but delightful. (1 John 5:3). Jesus' entire life was marked by holy poverty, extreme contempt, and severe persecution. Did He not come, "not to be ministered unto, but to minister, and to give his life a ransom for many" (Mat 20:28)?

The desire to excel others and be considered important is a natural tendency, but the spiritual person is drawn to the humility of the Redeemer and desires to be regarded as nothing in this world. The carnal man, driven by the inclinations of corrupt nature who has not learned from Christ's humility, meekness, and love, considers it foolish to live as Jesus lived. Believing instead that only those who indulge their desires and satisfy their every whim are truly wise. Such people are trapped in darkness and ignorance, blinded by their own selfishness, and the more they live in the devil the more they think their life is the happiest it can be, and congratulate themselves in their own folly. Following the light of carnal wisdom, these deluded wretches are so deceived that they not only deceive themselves but also lead others to the same ruin.

Those whose minds have been enlightened by the true light of Christ are shocked and horrified when they behold the pretension and vanity of this world; the ambition and pride; the wrath and revenge; the intemperance and self-indulgence that characterize the carnal life. They exclaim "Oh, how far from Christ is all this! How far from true repentance and knowledge of Jesus is the person who behaves like this! How far from the nature and disposition of a child of God! They are still dead in sin and slaves to the devil." Those who do not imitate the life of Christ are a stranger to true repentance; they are not a Christian or a child of God; they are utterly ignorant of Jesus Christ.

God's purpose in creating temporal things was to meet man's physical needs. It is fitting that these things be used for this purpose and that we receive them from God with gratitude and humility and use them with fear and trembling. The things of this world are God's property, not intended for our revelling nor to be indulged for worldly pleasure, but for His own profit and praise. When it comes to wealth, food, and clothing that are not essential, they are left to us as a means of testing our character. The manner in which these things are used when we have them reveals our disposition towards God. When we begin to stray from God, it is very easy to fall into the temptation to indulge in worldly pleasures. Will we remain faithful to God when surrounded by earthly possessions, keeping our eyes fixed on those things that are to come, or will our love for God be set aside for the love of the things of this world. Do we place our affections on a fading earthly paradise instead of that which is permanent and heavenly?

The pleasures of the world are the fruits of a forbidden tree that God warns us not to partake of lest, our minds being drawn to them, we eventually lose all taste for anything else, and find ourselves captivated by earthly things. By indulging the flesh, these people convert food, drink, clothing etc. into snares that turn them away from God. Man will be held accountable for those choices on judgment day. Man will be without excuse on that day because he will be rewarded according to his own will. This principle is echoed in the words of Moses, who solemnly declared to the Israelites, "I call heaven and earth to witness this day against you that I have set before you, life and death, blessing and curse. Now choose life, so that you and your descendants may live" (Deut. 30:19).

It is the duty of every true Christian to consider himself a stranger and pilgrim in this world; and he is required to use earthly blessings to supply his essential needs, not as a means of satisfying his selfish desires or depraved cravings. We should not set our affections on these earthly things, but on Him alone who is able to satisfy our needs. Otherwise, we expose ourselves to dangerous temptations, and with Eve, eat daily of the forbidden tree. A true Christian's focus is not on worldly concerns or material indulgences, for their inner gaze is fixed on the bread that endures unto eternal life. They are not concerned with fancy clothes, outward adornments or luxurious living, but rather aspire to obtain the adornment of a meek, humble and contrite spirit in the inward man that they may obtain glorified bodies, and be clothed in the divine light. In short, all the things that please the natural man in this world are, to a genuine Christian, only trials and temptations to be resisted, attractions to sin and snares of death that constantly test his virtue.

No matter how pleasant and beneficial something may appear to us, whatever we use or indulge in, to gratify our flesh without the fear of God, is a poison to our soul. Yet instead of striving to understand the forbidden tree of worldly pleasures and their consequences, we give ourselves up to a careless and thoughtless lifestyle, to the desires of the flesh without realizing that these desires are the forbidden tree. On the other hand, the Christian uses all things in the fear of God, viewing themselves as a stranger and pilgrim on the earth. They avoid every kind of excess in food, drink, clothing, homes, and other things of this life, lest by misusing them they offend Christ and fellow Christians. They will not even glance at the forbidden tree, lest they fall prey to its temptation. Instead, with the eyes of faith, they gaze steadfastly on the future glory of the soul, and for its sake, they resist the cravings of their corrupt nature.

What does it benefit the body that in this world it indulges in its desires and pleasures, only to be consumed, after a little while, by worms and stripped of its enjoyments? "Naked," says Job, "came I out of my mother's womb, and naked shall I return thither." (Job 1:21). We come into this world with a naked, weak, poor and needy body, which is ultimately the spoil of death. Whatever shelter, goods, food and drink we may have at death, along with our bodies and life itself is forever forfeited. What can be more wretched and poor, more naked and miserable, than man when he dies if he is not clothed with Christ's righteousness, and has life and treasure in heaven?

As we are admittedly strangers and pilgrims here, and must leave behind us every earthly enjoyment, let us not burden our souls with things that we cannot carry out of this world. Is it not absurd to heap up riches for a frail body that will be destroyed, and miss out on enjoying the riches of heaven? (Luke 12:20, 21). Remember that there is a better world, with a new body and new life. God sees us as pilgrims and strangers on this earth, even though it does not appear so to others (Ps. 39:12; Lev. 25:23). "Ye are," saith the Lord, "strangers and sojourners with me," that is, "before my eyes, although ye may not remember it."

If so, it will become apparent to us when we compare the visible with the invisible world, the earthly tabernacle with the heavenly, and things that are frail and perishing, with those that are lasting and eternal, that our country and our home must be elsewhere. This comparison will give us a deeper understanding of time and eternity, and lead us to see with the eye of faith, those things that are hidden from the unthinking masses.

It is from a lack of reflection on this matter that many are complacent and unruly in their behaviour, indulging in earthly pleasures and becoming consumed by greed and worldly worries. As a result, the majority of humanity, despite their keen business acumen and shrewdness in worldly pursuits, remain oblivious and insensitive to the concerns of their eternal soul. They become so enamoured with this life that they consider it to be the most delightful, the best, and the noblest of all, while the true Christian views it as a temporary exile, a valley of tears, a place of misery, and a dark prison.

As a result, those who love this world and seek their happiness in it are no wiser than beasts. They live and die like animals (Psa 49:12, 20). They are totally blind in regard to the inward man, never considering eternal matters. They find no joy in God, but only on the low and sordid pleasures offered by this world. They seek rest and comfort in the things of this world. After, through much effort, they obtain their desires, they sit back and congratulate themselves about their possessions. Oblivious to the tremendous concern of their eternal salvation, they are most wretched and miserable. Contently trapped in ignorant darkness, they will soon be swept away to death and damnation (Luke 1:79).

To gain a deeper understanding of our pilgrimage on earth, we should constantly reflect on the example left by Jesus Christ, and diligently follow Him in both His actions and His teachings. He has set before us a perfect model of universal holiness. As our captain and guide, we should strive to emulate His life and character. Go then, and look to Him, who despite being the greatest of all men, chose to live a life that was humble, poor, devoid of worldly honours, wealth, and pleasures – the very things that this world idolizes. All these things, which the world sacrifices to obtain, the Lord contemned in saying, "He had not where to lay his head." (Matt. 8:20).

David's character, before he became king, was likewise poor and despised. And even after he was crowned, he considered all his royal splendour as nothing compared to the eternal life and kingdom of God that he had been called to. He wrote, "How amiable," says he, "are thy tabernacles, O Lord of hosts! My soul longeth, yea, even fainteth for the courts of the Lord; my heart and my flesh crieth out for the living God."—"A day in thy courts is better than a thousand" (Ps 84:2,10). It is as if he said, "I may have a kingdom, people under my rule, kingly palaces, and the fortress of Zion but what are these compared to your sanctuary, O Lord of hosts?" Likewise, Job found comfort in his Redeemer. (Job 19:25).

The apostles, including Peter and Paul, did not seek the riches of this life. Instead, they focused on having riches in heaven. As a result, they freely adopted the despised life of Christ, walking in His love, humility, and patience. Rejecting the earth and triumphing over the temptations of this world, they prayed for those who cursed them, thanked those who reproached them and blessed those who reviled them (1 Cor. 4:12; Acts 5:41). When they were persecuted, they glorified God; when scourged, they were immovably patient, professing that "through much tribulation they must enter into the kingdom of God" (Acts 14:22); and when slaughtered, they prayed (with Christ), "Father, forgive them" (Luke 23:34); "lay not this sin to their charge." (Acts 7:60). On one hand, they were dead to all wrath and revenge; to bitterness, ambition and pride, to the love of the world, and of their own life also; while on the other they lived in Christ and in His love, meekness, humility, patience, and resignation. Those who live in this way are truly alive in Christ through faith.

To those who love the world, this exemplary way of life is unfamiliar, as they do not live in Christ or know that the truth is in Him. Instead, they remain dead in their sins, dead in anger, hatred, envy, greed, pride and revenge. Despite their boasts, as long as this remains, they remain in a state of unrepentance and have not been transformed by faith in Jesus. In contrast, true disciples of Christ recognize that it is their duty to follow in the footsteps of their divine Master (1 Peter 2:21) and conform to His life, which is the ultimate pattern of all virtue and goodness. The life of Christ serves as their guidebook, from which all solid and substantial learning about living and doctrine is derived. These individuals echo the apostle's words, "We look not at the things which are seen, but at the things which are not seen; for the things which are seen are temporal, but the things which are not seen are eternal" (2 Cor 4:18). Together with holy men of old they say, "Here have we no continuing city, but we seek one to come." (Heb 13:14).

Reviewing these points, in this world we are clearly only strangers with no permanent home. This suggests that we were not created solely for earthly pursuits, but rather there remains for us another country and other dwellings, which we should not hesitate to gain even if we must sacrifice a hundred worlds, or even life itself. The true Christian constantly thinks about these subjects with pleasure and it is his joy that here he has no permanent city but one waits for him in heaven. How sad is the condition of those who, consumed by worldly pursuits, burden their souls by the crushing weight of earthly vanity, exposing themselves to eternal destruction?

Chapter 10. Christian Warfare

I see another law in my members, warring against the law of my mind.—Rom. 7:23.

The two opposite principles in the heart of the real Christian are spoken of by the apostle under different names, viz.: the spirit of God and the Spirit of the world; the inward man and the outward man (2 Cor. 4:16); the new man and the old man (Eph 4:22-24); the law of the mind and the law of the members (Rom. 7:23); and the flesh and they spirit. "The flesh," he says, "lusteth against the Spirit, and the Spirit against the flesh." (Gal. 5:17). When the old man is crucified, he does not instantly die but lingers, struggling to regain control and will reassert himself if, by lack of constant watchfulness and prayer, he is not kept under subjection. This is a great threat to all who have at one time "tasted of the heavenly gift and made partakers of the Holy Ghost." (Heb 6:4). Believing themselves to have attained (Phil 3:12-14), they no longer fear for their souls (Heb 4:1) and, becoming complacent, they allow themselves to be deceived by the old man's self-assurance and self-esteem who regains control of their soul (Mat 24:43). Becoming again entangled and overcome by the spirit of this world they are worse off than in the beginning unless they return to repentance. (2 Pet 2:20)

We have already noticed what is meant by the old man, namely, self-will, self-love, self-interest, self-pleasing, self-esteem, self-honour, self-assurance, self-confidence, self-sufficiency, self-justification, and self-righteousness, which is manifested in pride, stubbornness, selfishness, covetousness, wrong doing, anger, impatience, hostility, hatred, etc. All this must die in the Christian, if the new man is ever to arise in him and be renewed day by day. Few understand how insidious and deceitful the perverse spirit and corrupt nature of the old man is, let alone, earnestly struggle against it. But if we are ever to save our souls from eternal ruin, we must die to our sinful nature and its restless workings.

You cannot be clothed with the humility of Christ unless your natural pride is first overcome. You cannot feel love for Christ's poverty unless your avarice and love for the world are first defeated. You will not be able to follow Christ's example of despising vanity and pride or endure the shame of His cross until ambition is eradicated from your heart. Similarly, you will not be able to express the meekness and patience of Jesus in your life until your vengeful spirit is inwardly mortified. The new man arises in proportion to the dying of the old man. As, by the grace of God, pride loses its influence, humility takes its place; as wrath subsides, meekness emerges; covetousness is replaced by trust in God; and the love of the world is supplanted by the love of God. As this transformation occurs, the renovation of the new man unfolds. This is the fruit of the Holy Spirit: practical and living faith (Gal 5:22). This is Christ in us, this is the new commandment, and obedience to Christ. This is the result of the new birth in us. To be a true child of God, we must live in this way, for only those who do so can claim to be one.

When the Spirit of God conquers the flesh, and overthrows its carnal spirit, then man lives in the new nature and is in God and in Christ; but when the flesh vanquishes God's Spirit, and regains the upper hand, then man lives in the devil and in the old nature; he is under the dominion of the spirit of world, and without the kingdom of God, and, consequently, is said to be carnal. And "to be carnally minded is death." (Rom. 8:6). Solomon says, "He that ruleth his spirit, is better than he that taketh a city." (Prov. 16:32). It is your choice of what spirit controls you. If, then, you want to be an overcomer, and gain an immortal victory, conquer yourself by faith; subdue your urges, mortify your pride, suppress your ambition, and destroy every undue desire which assails you; and by doing so you overthrow the kingdom of Satan, who, by means of such sins, rules in the world. Many have become famous by the capture of towns and cities but how few are they who, in a higher sense, may be called conquerors of the world! This contest, even though it brings various trials and difficulties, will result in a glorious victory and a heavenly crown: "Be thou faithful unto death," saith the Captain of our salvation, "and I will give thee a crown of life." (Rev. 2:10). The Bible says, "This is the victory that overcometh the world, even our faith." (1 John 5:4). What does it mean to overcome the world? It is primarily talking about the world within us. Overcome yourself, and then you will have victory over the world.

Some might ask, "If I struggle with sin and am swept away against my will, does that mean since the apostle John's says, "The one who commits sin is from the devil." (1 John 3:8) that I am excluded from being a child of God? To this, we must respond: If you feel the inner conflict between the Spirit and your flesh, and you are troubled that you sometimes act in ways you would not want to, it is evidence that despite your weaknesses, your faith and God's spirit are struggling against your flesh and opposing it. Even the apostle Paul acknowledged this internal warfare in believers when he wrote, "I see another law in my members warring against the law of my mind (that is, against the new, inward man), and bringing me into captivity to the law of sin which is in my members" (Rom 7:23). This sometimes caused him to do things he did not want to do. He had the will to do good, but he wasn't always able to do it; however, he could easily do what he did not want to do. Hence, he lamented, "Oh wretched man that I am! Who will deliver me from this body of death?" (Rom 7:24). This agrees with what Christ himself said: "The spirit is willing, but the flesh is weak." (Mat 26:41; Mark 14:38).

We should not become discouraged because we are imperfect and hindered by weaknesses that impede our progress in the divine life. Instead, we should be motivated to strive with greater earnestness for the desired goal. No matter how strongly the old man resists, he has been sentenced to death and must surely die. We should eagerly desire, pray, strive and study, for the kingdom of Christ to be established within us and for the kingdom of Satan within to be dismantled. (1 John 3:9; Eph 2:5). Our goal and efforts, our heartfelt longing and prayers, should be to constantly mortify the old man through daily repentance. The more we die to ourselves, the more Christ lives in us, the more corruptions are removed by the spirit of God and the more divine grace possesses the heart.

As the flesh is crucified, so the spirit is proportionately quickened; as the works of darkness are put off, the armour of light from above is put on; and in the same degree as the outward man perishes, the inward man is strengthened and renewed. (2 Cor 4:16; Col. 3:5). The decrease of the carnal life is the increase of the spiritual and divine. As the inclinations of self-love, self-assurance, self-exaltation, ambition, wrath, selfishness, and self-indulgence are weakened and subdued, so opposite dispositions of the Holy Spirit are invigorated and raised. The farther a man departs from the world, from "the lust of the flesh, the lust of the eyes, and the pride of life," (1 John 2:16) the more do God, Christ, and the Holy Spirit enter into the heart and dwell there. And, on the other hand, the more nature, flesh, darkness, and the spirit of the world reign in man, the less of grace, light, the Holy Spirit, God and Christ is there to be found in him.

It is the experience of all the saints that they all have sin, according to the word of the apostle John, "If we say that we have no sin, we deceive ourselves." (1 John 1:8). It is not, however, individual sins that are repented of that condemn a man, but the reigning of sin. The apostle Paul says, "There is therefore now no condemnation to them which are in Christ Jesus, who walk not after the flesh, but after the Spirit," (Rom. 8:1); that is, who do not permit their flesh with its carnal spirit to rule over them. Those who are not truly born again do not experience this combat between their flesh and the Holy Spirit. They remain at peace with the reign of their carnal spirit; they are pleased with themselves, being happy to remain its servants and are, consequently, damned; for "the law of the Spirit of life" hath not made them "free from the law of sin and death." (Rom. 8:2). This is illustrated in that the remnant of the Canaanites were permitted to dwell amongst the children of Israel, but not to have dominion over them (Josh. 16:10); and this led the Israel of God to feel their remaining imperfections.

This daily strife with the old man is an encouraging evidence of the existence of the new man; for it plainly indicates that there are two contending principles within you. The land of Canaan cannot be gained without war: but when the flesh, like the Canaanite of old, invades the territories of the spirit, the spiritual and true Israel must not permit it to take root, but, by the grace of God, we must collect new strength in Christ, and rise again from our fall by true repentance and confession, and earnestly implore Jesus, our true Joshua, to vanquish the spiritual Canaanite, the enemy of our soul, for us and in us.

For those who still struggle with their moral weaknesses and find it difficult to do what they want to do, I encourage them to cling to Jesus with sincere repentance and humility, and cover their mistakes with Christ's perfect obedience. It is only when a man forsakes his sin and, by daily repentance, strives against it, making amends for past mistakes, and takes steps to prevent future temptations, that the benefits of Christ's sacrifice become effective. But as long as man remains unbroken in heart because of his sinfulness; while he continues to gratify the unholy inclinations of the flesh, nothing can be more absurd than for him to suppose that Christ's merits can benefit him. How can the sacrifice of Christ be effective for someone who tramples upon it? (Heb 10:29).

Today, many people claim to be Christian even though they only do the bare minimum of what it entails. They are controlled by the unclean spirit of this world, not that of Christ. (Eph. 2:2). As a result, Jesus Christ is effectively denied, disrespected, blasphemed, crucified and, as it were, cast out from the sight of men as dead. The apostle Paul explicitly states that some people "crucify the Son of God afresh." (Heb 6:6). They call themselves after His name, and honour Him with their lips; and yet, by their unchristian behaviour, utterly reject and deny Him. It is rare to find someone who reflects Christ's holy, humble, and exemplary life; and, no matter how loudly they profess faith and doctrine, wherever the life of Christ is absent, Christ Himself is absent. For the Christian faith without a Christian life is a tree without fruit. True faith works by love (Gal. 5:6); and wherever it is found, there Christ dwells, with all His divine graces and virtues. (Eph. 3:17).

But when these are not expressed in the lives of those who profess His doctrine, Christ Himself is denied. As Jesus said, "Whoever denies me before others, I will also deny before my Father and the angels" (Mat 10:33, Luke 12:9). When by our lives we choose to sin against Jesus and resist the Holy Spirit, we are denying Him just as much as those who renounce Him outright. The apostle Paul warns that some people "profess that they know God, but in works deny him" (Titus 1:16). Christ is just as denied by the self-interested, self-assured, self-justifying, and self-honouring life of one who professes faith as He is by the verbal rejection of the reckless sinner. They will cry "Yea, yea," and "Lord, Lord!" (Matt. 7:21), but their true intentions are betrayed by their behaviour. They pretend to be children of the Father, but do not, in any respect, obey His will. They are worse than unbelievers. They are those that the apostle Paul describes as: "Having a form of godliness, but denying the power thereof." (2 Tim. 3:5). This hypocrisy is illustrated in Jesus' parable of the two sons, who were commanded to work in their father's vineyard. One son openly refused, saying "I will not," while the other son pretended to obey, saying "I'll go, sir," but did not actually go (Mat 21:28-30). Both open rebellion and pretended obedience are no different to God. Those who claim to be Christian but do not live like Christ will be denied by the Saviour Himself when He says to them: "I never knew you: depart from me, ye that work iniquity." (Matt. 7:23).

If we examine the conduct of most people including Christians today by the standards of Christ's teachings and example, we'll soon realize that it is largely unchristian and contrary to His example. Their lives are marked by an insatiable desire for wealth and status; love of the world, self-love, self-honour, and self-seeking. The life of Christ is opposed to all this, it proceeds from a different spirit having different values and priorities. If it is true that those who are not with Christ are against Him, and those who do not do God's will are in rebellion against Him, then most people who claim to be Christians are actually opposed to Him. Very few people actually are of one soul, one will, one mind and one spirit with Christ; yet only those who are can be His disciples. The apostle Paul emphasizes this when he writes about having, "the mind of Christ" (1 Cor. 2:16) and also. "Let this mind be in you which was also in Christ Jesus." (Phil. 2:5). Those who do not have this mind are not with Christ, but against Him. No matter what a man's profession and belief, he who is against Christ in his life and actions is most certainly an antichrist. (1 John 2:18).

Where then can we find true Christians among so many unchristian disorders all around us? Where can we find those that are seeking to be restored into the image of Christ rather than just avoiding the consequences of their sins? Where can we find those who, walking in the spirit of repentance, have true faith, rather than just presuming on God? How fitting that Jesus called them "a little flock" (Luke 12:32). The prophet Isaiah compared the church to a solitary cottage in a vineyard and to a wasted city (Isaiah 1:8). Micah lamented "Woe is me, for I am as when they have gathered the summer fruits, as the grape-gleanings of the vintage: there is no cluster to eat: my soul desires the first ripe fruit. The good man is perished out of the earth; and there is none upright among men." (Mic 7:1, 2; See also Ps. 74:19; 102:7).

God alone knows where and who these are, but wherever they are, be assured that Christ is with them, and in them, "alway, even unto the end of the world." (Matt. 28:20) He says to them; "I will not leave you comfortless, I will come unto you." (John 14:18). Christ knows who are His, and He watches over them with never-ceasing and distinguishing care. "The foundation of God standeth sure, having this seal, The Lord knoweth them that are his." But who *are His*? The answer is immediately provided: "Let everyone that nameth the name of Christ depart from iniquity." (2 Tim. 2:19). Whoever is not willing to obey this command, and does not desire to be restored into His humble, self-denying image should find another name that aligns with their conduct, and not claim to be a Christian until, through the faith of Jesus and continual repentance, they imitate His holy life.

Book II: Understanding Christianity

An analysis of fundamental Christian doctrines, in the light of the words of scripture and reason.

Isa 1:18 Come now, and let us reason together, saith the LORD.

Ps 32:9 Be ye not as the horse, or as the mule, which have no understanding.

Understanding Christianity

Introduction

Falling Away

With 2.4 billion or so people who currently consider themselves to be Christians, have you ever wondered what Jesus meant when he declared: "Nevertheless when the Son of man cometh, shall he find faith on the earth?" (Luke 18:8). Given what He said about the strait gate (Matt 7:13), He clearly was not talking about finding many who believe in Him or who are members of some Christian church. To explain the point of His question Jesus followed it up with the parable of the Pharisee and the publican (Luke 18:10-14). He meant that at His return, there will be many who believe in Jesus, are confident they have a good relationship with Him and expect to obtain His blessing, but will not be accepted by Him. Jesus further explained that when He returns many will presume that their faith in Christ and their Christian behaviour will grant them entry into the kingdom of heaven but He will reply, "Depart from me, I never knew you," to their cries of "Lord, Lord." No matter how confident one's belief is, how sincere one's hope is and how firm one's trust in Him is, Jesus will not recognise those as constituting true faith. We are left to wonder why that might be: is it because faith is more than belief, hope and trust, or because our understating of Christianity is wrong, or something else?

The answer is found in the apostle Paul's warning that the faith of many will be in vain because they have forgotten what he originally preached to them in 1 Cor 15:2. In another place He explained that the time would come when there would be a general falling away from the faith that was once delivered to the saints:

> 2Thess 2:3 there [will] come a falling away first, and that man of sin [will] be revealed, the son of perdition;

Not a falling of individuals away from the forms of Christianity, but a falling away of Christians from true Christianity as represented by the faith of Jesus, enabling the man of sin to:

> 2Thess 2:4 sit in the temple of God, shewing himself that he is God.

This watered down faith enables not just the MAN of sin to sit in the church of God and claim to be God, but any and all sinners can also sit comfortably in the church of God thinking themselves to have attained eternal life and thereby become, as it were, like god. However, Jesus warns that just as He cast the first sinners out of the Garden of Eden, He will cast out all sinners from his presence, irrespective of their presumed faith.

> **Jude 1:3** Beloved… it was needful for me to write unto you, and exhort you that ye should earnestly contend for the faith which was once delivered unto the saints.

Understanding the nature of this falling away is important so as not to be misled about what it entails. It is not the result of some wonder working deceiver in the last days, but has been developing gradually, almost imperceptibly, since the first century and has continued unabated until today (2 Thes 2:7).

Creeping Compromise

In its original form, Christianity presented a radical challenge from the tired religious philosophies of the day. In contrast to the self-serving desire for happiness in the present life and the hope of a better existence in the afterlife attained through outward beliefs, devotions, moral obligations, and sacred rituals of the other religions, Christianity focused on an inner transformation of the soul that transcends suffering in this life and even death. Heaven itself was not something to be coveted or selfishly grasped at, but received according to God's will as a means of further glorifying Him.

The power that attended the preaching of the gospel drew to it many who were selfishly seeking after miracles like Simon Magus (Acts 8:9-20). These cared little for the self-denying faith of Jesus but, nevertheless, wanted to enjoy Christ's blessings, popularity, power and financial benefits. Having a form of godliness they crept into the church and sought places at the highest seats in the church (Luke 20:46; 3 John 1:10). From there they proceeded to teach their own version of the gospel that was more in line with their self-interest: an understanding that was rooted in the pagan philosophies from which they had come. It did not take long for them to corrupt the pure faith once delivered to the saints.

> **Gal 2:4** And that because of false brethren unawares brought in, who came in privily [stealthily] to… bring us into bondage.

In the book of Revelation, Christ warned His church to remember from where they had fallen and urged them to repent and return to the purity of the gospel (Rev 2:5). A few did but many others continued drifting away and took

Introduction.

Christianity as a whole along with them. Their descendants eventually lost sight of primitive Christianity altogether. While they repeated the same words and spoke about the same themes, they no longer meant the same things. Devotion displaced piety, selfishness overtook self-denial, presumption replaced faith, self-satisfaction replaced humility, sentimental indulgence replaced true love, and policy replaced honesty. Instead of profoundly transforming the heart of man, this modern Christianity satisfied itself with little more than superficial changes: Superficial faith, superficial repentance, superficial love, and superficial godliness. It sounded like the original Christianity on the surface but underneath it had become just like all the other self-seeking religions. No longer being capable of meaningfully transforming society, this "improved" Christianity, replaced conviction through the sword of the spirit, with coercion through the sword of the state.

All religions claim that happiness in the present and afterlife is contingent upon following their prescribed beliefs and practices, relying on self-interest to motivate their adherents. In this regard today's Christianity is no different. We see this expressed by the famous French mathematician and Catholic theologian Blaise Pascal (1623-1662) in what has become known as Pascal's wager. In it he argued that a rational person should live as though God exists and seek to believe in God. If God does not actually exist, such a person will have only a finite loss (some pleasures, luxury, etc.), whereas he stands to receive infinite gains (as represented by eternity in Heaven) and avoid infinite losses (eternity in Hell). From a selfish perspective, Pascal's wager is a compelling argument for Christianity. However in making this proposition he unwittingly exposes that Christianity has become fundamentally no different from all other religions. Modern Christianity has become just another flavour in the candy shop of religion, where each flavour claims to be the best at providing emotional comfort, meaning and purpose, a sense of belonging, identity and a means of dealing with guilt.

Primitive Christianity would never have made the impact on the world that it did had Jesus come to give us just a new recipe for the same self-serving dish of religion. Instead Christ's Gospel was radical: its motivation was not based on selfishness; it offered no sense of moralistic superiority; it promised no temporal benefits; it presented no grounds for complacency; it tolerated no presumption of righteousness; and it provided no basis for self-satisfaction. It was contrary to every instinct of human nature. To be a Christian meant to go against well accepted ideas and social norms and one's own self-interest.

Christianity in Decline

Today's popular Christianity is no longer the faith that was once delivered to the saints. After being reinterpreted in the first few centuries through the lens of pagan religious thinking, what little remained of it has been further degraded over the last few centuries by the influences of humanism, modern psychology and spiritualism under the guise of the New Age movement. These have made subtle but deep inroads into all branches of Christianity.

The result of all this, in marked contrast to its beginnings when it turned the world upside down, is that Christianity is in decline in all over the world, especially in its traditional strongholds. Like something that has passed its use by date, it seems to have nothing much to offer to the world but wishful thinking and bygone moralism. Why should we expect anything else? Why be a Christian when it provides few advantages over competing ideologies? Apart from some minor details, it is in full harmony with the core concepts of modern psychology, humanism and many of the key concepts of most other religions. This is why many Christian churches today sit empty, and others have largely become the hangout of socially deprived older people wanting to hold onto their past, or of young people seeking to feel good about themselves through mindless, musically induced emotional highs coupled with modern psychology, or of those who selfishly presume that their religious beliefs and practices will somehow obtain for them benefits they know they have no rightful claim on.

In any case, today's Christianity is very different to the powerful, earnest, transformative and radical Christianity of the first century. Its understanding of what faith, grace, repentance, righteousness, etc., entail is very different from what it once was. As a consequence, no matter how sincerely or earnestly you believe yourself to be a Christian, unless you rediscover the Christianity of Jesus and put it into practice, He will not recognise you as His own when He returns to sort the sheep from the goats.

Saving Faith

What is Faith?

Faith is indispensable for the Christian, because "without faith it is impossible to please God" (Heb 11:6). The problem is that many Christians do not have real faith, nor even know what it is. Do not be shocked by this statement. When Jesus was on earth, He complained that His closest disciples only had a little faith, while commending complete strangers for having great faith. He also wondered whether after the gospel had been preached in the entire world (Matt 24:14) He would find any faith at His return (Luke 18:8).

Now many people like to quote Hebrews 11:1 to explain what faith is but this verse does not define faith; it only says that faith is an agent for making things that do not exist become a reality. It does not tell us what that agent is. Perhaps this is why people like using this verse to define faith: because it allows them to presume it to be whatever they want.

Dictionaries will define faith as some combination of belief, trust, hope, confidence, a religious persuasion, etc. You might say it is a confident religious belief that elicits a certain response. For example, the devils' belief in Christ's second coming and the fate of the wicked is not faith because it does not inspire them to trust or hope in God. Jesus, however, warned us through various parables that there will be many who have confidently believed in Him and have trusted and hoped that their faith will gain them entry into heaven, which will nevertheless be turned away. For example, the five foolish virgins and those who will in the last day cry out "Lord Lord we have preached in thy name and in thy name done wonderful works" to whom He will say depart from me. (Mat 7:22; 25:11). In 70AD the Jews confidently believed that God would not allow Jerusalem to be destroyed and, hoping and trusting in God's salvation, defied the Romans to the end. They certainly had a confident religious belief that elicited hope and trust. But was that belief, faith, or presumption?

Consider Romans 3:28 where it says that "a man is justified by faith." If faith is simply, one's belief, then this verse tells us that a man is justified by his own belief which makes him self-justified. His confidence is not in Christ but in his own belief about Christ. He believes himself saved by virtue of his self-confidence. Such belief is the opposite of faith.

Consider the dictionary definition of faith in the experience of Christ's apostles; they had a close personal relationship with Jesus, daily walking and talking with Him. They witnessed his miracles and, in His name, performed miracles themselves (Mark 3:14-15; 6:7, 13). They were convinced He was the Messiah. Did they believe and have confidence in Jesus' saving power and did it elicit in them hope and trust? Most certainly. Perhaps more than anyone else who has known Jesus Christ?

Yet, you can do all that and more without having any real faith. The Bible says you are saved through faith (Eph 2:8) yet we know that at the time he was walking with Jesus, Peter was unsaved or unconverted (Luk 22:32). Then there is Judas who also performed miracles in Jesus' name and believed, hoped, and trusted in Christ. Did he have faith or was it something else? So, we see that a confident belief in Jesus that elicits hope and trust, even when it involves a personal relationship that results in miracles, is not a good definition of faith.

Ye of Little Faith

Speaking of His disciples in general, Jesus repeatedly said they were of little faith (Matt 8:26; 14:31; 16:8; Luk 12:28), and:

> Matt 17:17-20 ... Jesus answered and said, O faithless and perverse generation, how long shall I be with you? how long shall I suffer you? ... Then came the disciples to Jesus apart, and said, Why could not we cast him out? And Jesus said unto them, Because of your unbelief: for verily I say unto you, if ye have faith as a grain of mustard seed, ye shall say unto this mountain, Remove hence to yonder place; and it shall remove; and nothing shall be impossible unto you.

On another occasion he said "if ye had faith as a grain of mustard seed, ye might say unto this Sycamine tree, Be thou plucked up by the root, and be thou planted in the sea; and it should obey you" (Luke 17:6). Jesus is not talking metaphorically here. He is talking about practical realities like opening the Red Sea, bringing water out of a rock, collapsing the walls of Jericho, making the sun to stand still, bringing fire down from heaven, bringing the dead back to life, and if God ordains it, moving literal trees and mountains. Jesus was saying that the disciples' faith was virtually non-existent: it was so weak as to be ineffective for any practical purpose.

Contrast the little faith of the apostles with the Canaanite woman from the

Saving Faith

area of Tyre and Sidon (Matt 5:21-28) or the centurion who came to Jesus because his servant was sick (Mat 8:5-12). Both were pagans having confused ideas about God and little understanding. Yet Jesus declared them to have great faith. There are two things that stand out from these examples: the urgency and perceived entitlement. We could call these two factors: present need and spiritual pride. Those with great faith had an urgent and present need of Christ. The disciples, on the other hand, looked forward to what Christ would do for them later when his kingdom was established (Mat 19:27-28). Faith is about having a need of God's saving power right now rather than needing his power at some future time.

The issue of perceived entitlement, or standing, with God is also important. Since they were not Jews, both the Roman centurion and the Canaanite woman (John 4:22) recognised that they had no standing at all with God that would entitle them to receive their requests. On the other hand, the Jews in general and the disciples in particular, believed, based on God's own word, that they had a privileged standing with God which entitled them to God's blessings. They were the chosen people to whom God had committed His oracles, promises and inheritance (Rom 3:1-2; 9:4). The centurion and Canaanite woman came to Christ boldly but also humbly, because they knew they had no rights before God. The disciples and Jews in contrast came expecting Christ's favour based on who they were, what they had done and what they believed.

Pharisees and Publicans

These issues are highlighted in the parable of the Pharisee and the Publican:

> Luke 18:10-14 Two men went up into the temple to pray; the one a Pharisee, and the other a publican. The Pharisee stood and prayed thus with himself, God, I thank thee, that I am not as other men are, extortioners, unjust, adulterers, or even as this publican. I fast twice in the week, I give tithes of all that I possess. And the publican, standing afar off, would not lift up so much as his eyes unto heaven, but smote upon his breast, saying, God be merciful to me a sinner. I tell you, this man went down to his house justified rather than the other: for every one that exalteth himself shall be abased; and he that humbleth himself shall be exalted.

Both were believers in God and trusted and hoped in Him. We are not told if one was more of a sinner than the other. The Pharisee had no real faith as it was unable to draw grace from God. The Publican did obtain grace because his faith was true. Again, we see that the Pharisee had no present need of God's help: he was proud of his spiritual condition, feeling that he had a good standing with God. The publican in contrast came ashamed of his spiritual condition: in urgent need he humbly begged for God's mercy knowing he did not deserve it.

Faith vs Presumption

On another occasion Christ's disciples asked him to increase their faith. Jesus responded by telling them that faith was all about their attitude (Luke 17:5-10). He said that they should not expect any reward for having done a part of God's will but to realise that they need to do much more. "When ye shall have done all those things which are commanded you, say, we are unprofitable servants: we have done that which was our duty to do." Without a correct attitude it is not possible to have true faith (Luk 14:11; Jam 4:10,6; Mat 5:3). Paul says that we should realise that our estimation of our standing with God is proportional to how much faith we have: as spiritual pride increases, faith decreases.

> **Rom 12:3** every man [should] not to think of himself more highly than he ought to think; but... think soberly, according as God hath dealt to every man the measure of faith.

There are two words that characterise the attitudes of the Pharisee and the Publican. They are repentance and presumption. The Publican came to God in repentance. The Pharisee came to God in presumption. That is not to say that the Pharisee had never experienced any repentance. Just that he presumed that his current spiritual condition and, hence his standing with God, was good so he had no present need for repentance. So, we see that the degree of repentance one has is directly proportional to how much faith one has, and the more presumption one has the less faith one has. In other words, without repentance, there can be no faith but only presumption which is the counterfeit of faith.

Like faith, presumption is also a confident belief but one that is misguided and elicits a false hope and false trust. It leads one to expect a blessing when one is incurring a curse and to expect a reward when one is destined to be punished. It causes one to think that their religious observances and devotions are evidence of a good relationship with God when God does not

Saving Faith

hear them (Isa 59:1-2). For example, Judas presumed that his betrayal of Christ would not result in Christ's condemnation and death (Mat 27:3). Peter presumed that his belief in and love for Christ was such that he would die before denying Him (Mat 26:35). Peter presumed his relationship with Christ assured his place in the kingdom (Luke 22:23-24), yet he had not at that time met the condition to enter the kingdom of God (John 3:3). Was Peter's faith the greatest when he was boasting of how he would give up his life for Jesus or after his denial and repentance?

Many confirmed Christians, like Peter, presume that they are "saved" and have a good standing with Christ; that they are covered by His righteousness and are rich in God's spirit, while they are spiritually poor and blind and naked and in need of repentance (Rev 3:16-19). When Jesus commended the faith of the centurion, He said to his hearers, who had received the promise, were expecting to inherit it, and thought that their place in the kingdom was sure:

> **Matt 8:11-12** And I say unto you, That many shall come… and shall sit down … in the kingdom of heaven. But the children of the kingdom shall be cast out into outer darkness: there shall be weeping and gnashing of teeth.

Their belief was in vain. When Jesus comes again to separate the sheep from the goats and the wheat from the tares (Matt 13:24-30;14:46-50; 25:32), many who have believed, hoped and trusted in Jesus and confidently looked forward to his salvation will sadly find they have confused faith with presumption and also believed in vain (1 Cor 15:2). We ought to fear that our own faith is also not just presumption, as Paul said:

> **Heb 4:1** Let us therefore fear, lest, a promise being left us of entering into his rest, any of you should seem to come short of it.

Faith is not just a confident belief in God that elicits in us hope and trust. It is earnestly seeking God (Heb 11:6) in urgent need and recognizing our spiritual poverty in humility (Psa 10:17; Isa 66:2) and repentance. If you have no urgent need of God, or think you have by some means obtained an entitlement to God's blessings, then you have no real faith.

True Repentance

What is Repentance?

Many Christians like to claim that they are saved by faith alone, which is true if one realises, as we discovered in the previous chapter, that faith without repentance is nothing more than presumption. Sins cannot be pardoned by faith alone without repentance (Acts 2:38, 3:19; Mark 1:4; Luke 17:3-4, 24:47). Unfortunately, like faith, biblical repentance is not very well understood today. This is not surprising because even the apostle Peter, who had been a disciple of John the Baptist, and who had himself preached the gospel of repentance for years and baptized many with the baptism of repentance (John 4:1-2), had not truly experienced repentance himself nor really understood it. That is, until he was finally converted (Luk 22:32). True repentance is not only alien to the natural heart but, according to modern psychology, it is a mental illness to be avoided at all costs (1 Cor 2:14).

What is repentance? The dictionary defines repentance as feeling sorry for something you have done and wishing you had not done it. The words regret, guilt and remorse are often used to describe it. The Greek word translated as repentance literally means a change of mind. While the Hebrew word translated as repentance (נחם: nocham) primarily means to be sorry, some say it means turn back or turn around. Accordingly, they say repentance is turning from unbelief to obedience toward God. Is this true repentance? Was it true repentance when, the Israelites turned from their unbelief in God's promise and presumed to invade the land of the Amalekites after God had pronounced His sentence at their refusal to believe Him and enter Canaan (Num14:44), or was it a repentance to be repented of (2 Cor 7:10)?

Some say repentance is feeling remorse or regret over individual sins and turning away from those sins. Consider the case of Esau. He sold his birth right to Jacob and married Canaanite wives, but seeing the consequences of his actions, felt sorry and tried to remedy his mistake (Gen 27:34, 38; 28:8) but we are told that was not repentance (Heb 12:17). Consider Judas who, having realised that he had miscalculated in betraying Jesus, was sorry for having done so and tried to return the money he had been paid (Mat 27:3-5). Or Balaam who, after seeing the angel ready to slay him, was sorry for his actions and offered to turn back? All these were sorry for what they had done and tried to correct their mistakes to escape the inevitable consequences, yet their so-called repentance was not effective (2 Cor 7:10). The Bible singles them out as examples of the unrepentant. True repentance is not about seeking to avoid the consequences of sin. Whether the motivation is fear of legal consequences or consequences to a relationship, doing so is only selfish. Selfishness is not a fruit of the spirit but a lust of the flesh. Is the lust of the flesh the means by which God proposes to save man? Did not Jesus die so that we might escape the lusts of our flesh (1 Pet 4:2) and no longer live unto ourselves (1 Cor 5:15)?

Repent from What?

We cannot understand repentance without first understanding what we need to repent from. The Old Testament says that unless Israel repented, iniquity would be their ruin (Ezek 18:30) even though they kept the law (Rom 9:31) because God will punish the world not just for sin but also for iniquity (Isa 26:21; Isa 13:11). In Hebrew, different words are used for distinct types of wrong. The word translated as sin in the Old Testament (חַטָּאָה: chatta'ah) means only breaking the law while the word translated as iniquity (עָוֹן: ʿavon) means moral failure or depravity. Now God, who is not willing that any should perish, (1 Pet 3:9) sent his son Jesus "to call sinners to repentance" (Mat 9:13). The Greek root of the word translated as 'sinners' is (ἁμαρτία: amartia) which means any moral failing such as selfishness, pride, intemperance, etc, and includes the breaking or transgression of the law (1 Joh 3:4). The New Testament defines sin as not doing what is good when you know what is good (Jas 4:17). So, one can sin even without the law and perish (Rom 2:12). When it says "the wages of sin is death" (John 6:23), it means that any of our moral failings, not just breaking the commandments, can bring death.

We see this illustrated in the story of the rich young ruler who asked Jesus what he needed to do to inherit eternal life. Jesus told him that his keeping of the commandments was not enough, but he also had to give away all his riches, and thereby repent of his selfishness (Mat 19:16-22). We also see this in the parable of the five foolish virgins. They are not remorseless sinners. They sincerely believe the truth of the Bible (Ps 119:105), have heard and studied Christ's words, are waiting for the bridegroom, and are expecting to meet him in peace because they are chaste virgins. Suddenly realising they do not have enough oil in their lamps, they go out at midnight to purchase oil but when they return, they find the door shut and they are not permitted to enter the marriage feast (Mat 25:1-12). In talking about the shut door Jesus did not describe those that call Him Lord and want to come in as sinners or transgressors; instead, he called them workers of iniquity (Luke 13:25-28; Matt 7:22-23). That is, they are selfish, proud, indolent, covetous etc. Even though, according to the dictionary definition, we could say the foolish virgins selfishly repented of their mistake, it was not true repentance.

Since it is impossible to separate ourselves from our moral depravity, (Jer 13:23; 17:9; Rom 7:21) true repentance is not limited to our past unbelief nor individual acts of sin, but also extends to the inherent evil within ourselves. David's repentance was not just over his transgression, but over his corrupt nature, over his iniquities.

> **Ps 51:9-10** blot out all mine iniquities. Create in me a clean heart, O God; and renew a right spirit within me.

According to God, Job was a perfect and upright man. So much so that there was none like him in the earth. Yet when Job saw God, he abhorred himself and repented in dust and ashes (Job 42:5-6) It was not because he had committed sin as his 3 friends claimed, that he repented, but because when he saw God, he saw his own imperfect nature in the light of the purity and holiness of God. How could he do anything other than repent from himself?

True repentance is not a means for selfishly avoiding the evil consequences of our sins but is a godly sorrow (2 Cor 7:10) brought about by a recognition of and hatred of our own inward corruption, and a deep yearning for holiness in the inner man. It is distrusting ourselves and a constant, urgent desire to be free from our sinful natures. This repentance is not natural to the human heart: it a gift from God and one which all must obtain if they are to be saved.

Continual Repentance

When Jesus came preaching the gospel he said:

> **Mark 1:15** The time is fulfilled, and the kingdom of God is at hand: repent ye, and believe the gospel.

The words translated here as "repent" and "believe" have an active continual aspect in the Greek. What Jesus meant was that entry into the kingdom of God required spending the whole of your life repenting and believing: a continuous ongoing experience. Repentance is not the work of a moment: it

True Repentance

does not happen once, nor even from time to time, but it is and ongoing, lifelong work that must continue as long as the carnal nature remains. Just as we are to continually exercise faith, we must continually exercise repentance. The Bible says that the Christian life is but a continuation of the means by which we first receive Christ, who came to bring us repentance (Acts 5:31).

> **Col 2:6** As ye have therefore received Christ Jesus the Lord, so walk ye in him:

How do we receive Christ? Through repentance and faith. Both need to be continually exercised to walk the Christian life and escape the corruption that is in the world through lust (2 Pet 1:4).

> **Gal 5:16** This I say then, Walk in the Spirit, and ye shall not fulfil the lust of the flesh.

The role of the Holy Spirit is also to bring us to repentance (Joh 16:7-8) so, we cannot walk in the Spirit without being filled with repentance. Accordingly, the lusts of the flesh cannot be overcome without continual repentance. No one can progress in the Christian Walk by trying to hop along on the lone leg of faith and those who attempt to do so are spiritual cripples. How do we know we are walking in the spirit? Because we are experiencing continual repentance.

> **Heb 3:14** we are made partakers of Christ, if we hold the beginning of our confidence steadfast unto the end;

If repentance is the evidence of the working of the Holy Spirit in our hearts it is therefore the beginning of our Christian confidence. Only those who steadfastly hold onto their repentance until the end have any part with Christ. Unfortunately, soon after Jesus returned to heaven the church seemed to have forgot that walking in Christ requires continual repentance and so He exhorted them saying "I have somewhat against thee" ...

> **Rev 3:3** Remember therefore how thou hast received and heard, and hold fast, and repent.

Today's Christians have also forgotten how they received and heard because the first of the ninety-five theses of the great reformer Martin Luther reads, "When our Lord and Master Jesus Christ said "Repent," he intended that the entire life of believers should be repentance. John Calvin in his Institutes (614-615) wrote: "Therefore, I think he has profited greatly who has learned to be very much displeased with himself, not so as to stick fast in this mire and progress no farther, but rather to hasten to God and yearn for him in order that, having been engrafted into the life and death of Christ, he may give attention to continual repentance. Truly, they who are held by a real loathing of sin cannot do otherwise."

The modern, popular gospel rejects the need for continual repentance, teaching that you can be saved in iniquity if you have remorse for breaking the law and desire to be saved from its penalty. They do not understand that no one can be saved from the penalty of sin unless one is first saved from sin, and no one can be saved from sin unless they are first saved from their iniquity. No one can be saved from iniquity unless they are continually walking in the spirit of true repentance. That is, no one can be saved unless they recognise and hate the depravity within their own hearts and are earnestly seeking to be freed from their sinful natures and yearn for holiness in the inner man. This is the only motivating power by which one can continually overcome himself, from where sin arises.

Rom 6:7 For he that is dead is freed from sin.

It is the only way that the old man can constantly be removed out of the away, so that the new man "created in righteousness and true holiness" may appear **(Eph 4:24)** "without which no man shall see the Lord" **(Heb 12:14)**. The Christian life is not about wandering around feeling assured that you are saved from the consequences of your sins, but about longing and struggling through God's grace to be saved from your carnal nature **(Rom 8:19-23)**.

The New Birth

You must be Born Again

It has been said that a text without the context is a pretext. Many people like to quote John 3:16 without its context and assume that their belief in their own salvation though Jesus is all that is necessary to be saved. However, they neglect the most important part: "verily, verily... unless a man be born again, he cannot see the kingdom of God." (John 3:3) Without the new birth, a man's belief cannot save him. The rich young ruler believed but was not saved (Mat 19:16-22), the devils believe but won't be saved (Jam 2:19), and we are told many will cry out "Lord Lord" in vain belief (1 Cor 15:2) but will not be saved (Mat 7:21). Their belief, hope and trust cannot save them unless they are born again.

The new birth or conversion, as it is sometimes called, is just as much a mystery for many today as it was when Jesus first mentioned it to Nicodemus. Many think it means a self-interested decision to turn from unbelief to belief, or to repurpose their lives based on the realisation, as per Pascal's famous wager, that one has infinitely more to lose if Christianity is true than if it is not. Others think one is born again when they are baptised (John 3:5). Is being born again just a decision to become a Christian; is it the result of baptism or is it something else altogether? Jesus made it clear that the new birth is not under the control of man, it is not the result of water baptism, nor any other decision of man. Instead, He compared it to the wind that comes and goes where and when it wants (John 3:8).

The only role of man in the new birth is the decision to accept Christ and learn of Him. However, coming to Christ in this manner is not the new birth but simply a precondition to it. The apostle Peter came to Jesus and walked and talked with Him daily for three years before he was converted. (Luke 22:32) Indeed, many others of his disciples were never born again and, like the rich young ruler, eventually turned away from Him (John 6:60, 66). Jesus told the parable of the sower to illustrate how one can accept the gospel seed without it ever bearing fruit (Matt 13:18-23). Yet, unless one first comes to Jesus, one will never understand the things of God and cannot be born again.

Another question many are confused about is the result of the new birth. Some think it is a change of legal status in heaven, from damned to saved, by means of their changed belief or participation in some sacrament. However, the new birth is not some theoretical or metaphorical fig leaf that covers our spiritual nakedness, but a practical reality. (1 Joh 2:4).

Others suppose it is a change of identity from lost to saved, (like a male who identifies as a female), based on external manifestations such as church attendance, works of charity, a show of humility, self-righteous expressions of moralism, or self-entitled boasts of unmerited favour. The new birth provides no such basis for self-deception; it does not matter if you identify as a Christian, it only matters what God identifies you to be, and He says, "many will say in that day Lord Lord ...And then will I profess unto them, I never knew you" (Matt 7:22-23).

Still others claim it is a metaphysical upgrade of their soul that somehow transforms them from sinners to saints while leaving the root of sin unchanged in them. However, the new birth does not make sinners suppose themselves to be saints, but rather makes self-supposed saints realise that they are sinners (Luke 18:10-14) and even the chief of sinners. (1 Tim 1:15)

In all these cases, the idea is that the new birth somehow entitles one to God's otherwise unmerited favour, preferential treatment, or another advantage that others do not enjoy. It is as if God, who is no respecter of persons, (Act 10:34) has special respect for those who claim to be born again so they are no longer subject to His judgement (which all must face) (Rom 14:10; 2 Cor 5:10).

Believers must be Born Again

To properly understand the new birth we need to understand that when Christ said, "you must be born again," He was not talking to an unbelieving gentile but to a devout Jewish leader, who not only believed in God but lived up to the scriptures as best he knew (Phil 3:5-6). He felt that, as a child of Abraham, he had a birth right to enter heaven as long as he continued to believe in and obey the God of Abraham.

The Jews well understood the metaphor of being born again since they used it to describe how a gentile could share in their birth right and be assured of salvation by becoming a Jew. When Jesus said that he must be born again, Nicodemus understood that to mean that he had to give up his Jewish birth right, his confidence on his standing with God and his expectation of God's blessings. It meant that he had to be something other than a Jew. He had to be in the same position as the despised Roman centurion whose servant was sick, the loathed Canaanite woman whose daughter was vexed by a devil, the repulsive Samaritan leaper, or the repugnant demoniac in the country of the Gadarenes. It meant he had to become as a gentile or Samaritan: condemned by God, undeserving of His blessings and destined to hell. It meant that he had to abandon all confidence based on who he was, what he did and what he believed and that his only hope was in humbly pleading for the mercy of God.

Jesus taught the same lesson in the parable of the Pharisee and the publican (Luke 18:10-14): God only hears those who abase themselves, realising that they have no more entitlement to His blessings than a lost sinner. God opposes those who esteem their spiritual attainments, but approves those who, having a low estimate of their spiritual attainments, come to Him recognising their spiritual need (Jam 4:6, 9-10). Being born again has little to do with deciding to believe in God and more to do with abandoning all illusions of our own goodness, abandoning our spiritual smugness, realising our spiritual poverty, and recognising our desperate, continual need of God's grace.

> Ps 34:18 The LORD is nigh unto them that are of a broken heart; and saveth such as be of a contrite spirit.
>
> Isa 57:15 For thus saith the high and lofty One that inhabiteth eternity, whose name is Holy; I dwell in the high and holy place, with him also that is of a contrite and humble spirit, to revive the spirit of the humble, and to revive the heart of the contrite ones.

A New Spirit within You

In this light we see that the new birth is a fundamental change of the spirit that is within you. It is a change from self-confidence to self-doubt, from self-satisfaction to self-abasement, from self-approval to self-condemnation. Since God is no respecter of persons, the Christian stands before God today in the same capacity as the Jew stood before Him 2000 years ago. Just as Jesus told a Jew, not a gentile, that he must be born again today, He is calling for Christians, not atheists or infidels, to be born again.

The new birth is the ongoing realisation that there is no more hope for the salvation of our Christian self than there is for the salvation of the atheist or infidel. It is to stop feeling secure of the supposed privileges of our Christian birth right. Our Christian beliefs, morals, good deeds, past repentance and past avoidance of sin gain for us no advantage before God whatsoever. The new birth is the realisation that only our continual pleading at the foot of the cross because of our desperate need for God's continued grace is of any value.

More than this, being born again is realising one's own wretchedness, it is a change of motivation; it is to stop seeking the glorification of self, whether in this life or the next, and seeking instead the glory of God even, if need be, at the cost of heaven (Exo 32:32). It is to cease living unto ourselves (1 Cor 5:15), to not seek our own good, but rather the good of others, beginning with God and ending with our neighbour. It is striving to not speak our own words nor do our own works, but to speak the words of Christ and do His works (John 14:10-11).

After having come to Christ and beholding His glory, the Holy Spirit strives against one's flesh, and one's flesh against the spirit (Gal 5:17; 4:29), and thus one gains a true knowledge of oneself. If one does not reject the witness of the Holy Spirit against oneself, the heart is broken, filling the soul with repentance, the mind is convicted of the need for self to be crucified with Christ (Gal 2:20; Mat 10:38), that the life of Christ and His holiness may take possession of the soul, and Christ's thoughts, desires, tastes, ambitions, affections, will, and reputation become one's own (Phil 2:5; Phil 2:7; Gal 5:24). Then as one accepts the Holy Spirit's call to fully surrender self as a living sacrifice to God (Rom 12:1); a new spirit takes possession of the heart (Eze 11:19) and one is born again.

A Spirit of Repentance

The unclean spirit of pride and presumption is replaced by a spirit of repentance, contrition, and spiritual humility. As the old man is crucified, the spirit which raised Christ up from the dead will dwell in us and make us to walk in newness of life: a life like that of Christ. Not a life of thinking we have attained (Phil 3:12) but a life of "prayers and supplications, with strong crying and tears" (Heb 5:7). There is an abandoning of one's self-image with all its presumed goodness, merit, and spiritual attainments. There is a dying to self: to self-righteousness, self-confidence, self-importance, self-satisfaction, self-approval, self-indulgence, self-assurance, and self-esteem. This must happen not just one time in the past, but daily (Luke 9:23; 1 Cor 15:31) since self will constantly try to regain control of the soul, until our carnal bodies are no

The New Birth

more. Self must die daily lest the old, unclean spirit returns and brings "with himself seven other spirits more wicked than himself and enter in" to the soul so that "the last state of that man is worse than the first" (Mat 12:45).

Without continual repentance, no one can be born again unless they are still born. Only through continual repentance and faith can the old spirit of presumption and pride be kept from resuming control of the soul. Only by continually crying out to "Him who is able to keep them from falling and present them faultless before the presence of his glory" (Jude 1:24), can the Spirit of Life be retained in the heart and keep one from falling away.

The devout Pharisee in the parable was unconverted: he was satisfied with his spiritual condition. Feeling assured of God's blessings, he felt no need for repentance. The ear of God is closed to the prayer of those who, like the Pharisee, presume themselves to be spiritually alive, while being spiritually dead. Maybe he did repent at some point in his life long ago, but the spirit of life had long departed from his soul. In contrast, the publican, coming to God in humble repentance with a broken and contrite spirit, showed that he had been born again and his prayer was heard.

Who you are, what you believe, what you do, or which group you belong to does not matter unless you are born again. You may have a form of godliness, a show of religion, but if you are spiritually satisfied, feel entitled and do not realise your own wretchedness, you are devoid of the spirit of life. You may claim to be spirit filled, but, unless you are filled with the spirit of brokenness, humility, and contrition, you are not converted. Examine yourself: are you alive by the spirit of God, or are you still born?

Rev 3:17, 16 Because thou sayest, I am rich, and increased with goods, and have need of nothing... I will spue thee out of my mouth.

The Kingdom of God

What is the Kingdom of God?

When Jesus came heralding the kingdom of God, the Jews thought He spoke about a political kingdom. When that did not materialise, others assumed He meant a religious organisation, where "they that exercise authority upon them are called benefactors" (Luke 22:25). Many evangelicals consider the kingdom of God to be an ideological kingdom which is made up of those who have a Christian ideology. The definition of what the specific ideology is required for citizenship in the kingdom varies. Jesus:

> **Luke 17:20 - 21** when he was demanded of the Pharisees, when the kingdom of God should come, he answered them and said, The kingdom of God cometh not with observation: Neither shall they say, Lo here! or, lo there! for, behold, the kingdom of God is within you.

Accordingly, the kingdom of God is not about being under the influence or authority of any kind of group of people, rather it is about being under the control and influence of God. It is about being under the realm of God instead of the realm of man. What are the realm of God and the realm of man?

The realm of man is constrained to those things he has control over. At the least, all men have control over their mind and their body. They may also have control over personal property to do with as their mind disposes and bodily potential permits. From the mind arises thoughts and from the body arises actions. In regard to man's pursuit of religion these thoughts are directed towards belief, trust, hope, and confidence, including mediation, and the works are directed towards devotion, charity, rituals, penance, law keeping and even psychedelic drug taking depending on the religion; whether it be Christianity, Hinduism, Buddhism, Islam or Shamanism, etc.

If the realm of man is depicted as a flat plane, the realm of God lies on a plane far above it. God's realm is not just a more expansive form of man's realm over which He has unlimited power. Its primary domain is spiritual. Not only is "God... a spirit" (Joh 4:24), but He is the "Father of Spirits" (Heb 12:9) and He disposes and rules over them. He "maketh his angels ministering spirits" (Heb 1:7) and "even the unclean spirits obey him" (Mar 1:27). God's realm is primarily spiritual because He created the physical earth and heaven to be the domains of His vassals; men and angels. What man perceives as spiritual and what God's spiritual reality is, are two different things. The realm of God is not some ethereal abode of disembodied spirits. By spiritual is meant character and personality coexisting with, and ruling over, physical matter. That is, God's realm primarily concerns the psyche, the inner self, of men and angels.

While God rules over all spirits, man cannot even rule over his own. Man has limited understanding or control of his spirit which comprises his attitudes, inclinations, propensities, temperament and character, and largely shapes his thoughts and actions unless overridden by deliberate choice. While he can moderate less agreeable aspects of his spirit, on his own, man can never completely escape its dispositions, resulting in the evil thoughts and actions of men. The spirit of man can never transcend its self-interest. It is an unclean, carnal spirit of selfishness and pride that is hostile to God's spirit.

1 Cor 2:11 For what man knoweth the things of a man, save the spirit of man which is in him?

While man is occupied with pursuing his own interests by exercising his mind and body, God is concerned with exercising his Spirit within the heart of men for their eternal benefit.

Religion in the realm of man

Ignoring the realm of God for now, man is nevertheless a religious creature. Man needs an explanation for the purpose of life, a moral compass and hope in regard to his destiny. The concept of good or evil demands religion since it cannot be logically explained without the existence of the divine. Science has no explanation for it; evolution has no need for it. Under the Darwinian theory of survival of the fittest, the idea of good vs evil in survival enhancing adaptations is meaningless since survival itself is ultimately meaningless.

Man seeks to resolve these questions through religion, be it theistic, pantheistic or atheistic. In the case of theism or pantheism man imagines that by exercising of his own mind and body he is able to intrude into the realm of God and launch his own spirit into eternal bliss. In this context we find a persistent debate about the role of one's actions in trespassing onto the realm of God. For some it is purely a matter of mind, while others say that it is a matter of mind and body. No one claims that it is possible to attain spirituality through exercise of the body alone without exercising the mind.

In Jesus' day this debate was carried on by Sadducees and Pharisees. Both believed they were destined to God's kingdom by virtue of God's unmerited favour towards Israel. The Sadducees believed that belief in expiatory sacrifices as described in the Law of Moses, was alone sufficient to fulfil their destiny. The Pharisees argued that both the mind and the body needed to be exercised: both faith, along with works resulting from that faith, such as fasting and keeping a myriad of religious laws and customs to ensure acceptance into God's kingdom. Neither of the two understood Jesus when He spoke about the kingdom of God and the requirements needed to enter it because His teachings were on an altogether different plane. He did not speak about the human realm, but the divine.

> **Isa 55:8 - 9** For my thoughts are not your thoughts, neither are your ways my ways, saith the LORD. For as the heavens are higher than the earth, so are my ... thoughts than your thoughts.
>
> **1 Cor 2:14** But the natural man receiveth not the things of the Spirit of God: for they are foolishness unto him: neither can he know them, because they are spiritually discerned.

When Jesus said to Nicodemus that unless a man be born of water and of the spirit he cannot see the kingdom of heaven, He was saying that entry into the kingdom of heaven does not depend on anything in the realm of man. Nothing the spirit of man leads him to believe, feel or do has any merit whatsoever. Only as God instils His own spirit in man can he enter into it.

> **John 3:5** Jesus answered, Verily, verily, I say unto thee, Except a man be born of water and of the Spirit, he cannot enter into the kingdom of God.
>
> **John 3:6** That which is born of the flesh is flesh; and that which is born of the Spirit is spirit.

Many believe that when Jesus said that a man must be born of water and the spirit He meant that man enters the kingdom of heaven by the ritual of baptism. They claim that by the act of baptism one somehow receives the Holy Spirit but the book of Acts shows that this is not so. Not all that were baptised received the Holy Ghost **(Acts 8:5, 12-16)**. There were others who received the Holy Ghost even without being baptised **(Acts 10:44-48)**. Of the multitudes that have since been baptised, few have been truly born of the spirit **(Mat 7:14)**.

Religion in the realm of God

The new birth is not a cooperation between the spirit of God and the spirit of man, but a replacement of the spirit by which man's hope for salvation is withdrawn from the realm of man and directed towards the realm of God. In explaining to Nicodemus what He meant about being born again, Jesus said;

> **John 3:7-8** Marvel not that I said unto thee, Ye must be born again. The wind bloweth where it listeth, and thou hearest the sound thereof, but canst not tell whence it cometh, and whither it goeth: so is every one that is born of the Spirit.

Being born again is not an initiative of man but of God. Only as God dethrones the spirit of man and places his Holy Spirit in its place can man have a part in the kingdom of heaven. It lifts man out of the realm of man and into the realm of God. This is not to say that there is absolutely nothing man can do to partake of the kingdom of God. There is; but all he can do is to seek for it **(Mat 6:33, Jer 29:13)**. Since the kingdom of God is within you, not without, you must seek for it within yourself. This does not mean searching for it in your own ideas or feelings, nor in the wisdom of man, but in the foolishness of this world **(1 Cor 3:19)**. "There is a way that seems right unto a man, but the way leads unto death." **(Prov 14:12)** and "the heart is deceitful above all things and desperately wicked." **(Jer 17:9)**. It means to search within your conscience illuminated by the Word of God, and the still small voice of the Holy Spirit within your heart. **(1 Kgs 19:12)** As "God has revealed it to us by his Spirit" **(1 Cor 2:10-12)**; "The Holy Ghost is also a witness to us" **(Heb 10:15)**. Being beyond the realm of man, it is only in self-doubt and self-criticism that man has any possibility of finding the kingdom of heaven **(2 Cor 13:5)**. This is why "few there be that find" the way into the kingdom.

Having found it, there is nothing one can do to enter into it but to surrender oneself, permitting the Spirit of God to take control of one's mind and body. Surrendering oneself means abandoning all self-interest, self-confidence, self-sufficiency, self-exaltation, and self-love, etc. The spirit of God does not intrude into the stronghold of the spirit of man. By turning away from our own spirit we open the door for the kingdom of God to annex the territory of our soul. It is not about you getting hold of God's spirit, but of His spirit getting hold of you. God's Spirit is like the wind which travels from places of high pressure to areas of low pressure or like water flowing downhill. The spirit flows down from heaven to the places where the spirit of man is most subdued since "blessed are the poor in spirit" **(Mat 5:3)**. Jesus explained the kingdom of God with many parables. The parables of the pearl of great price, the treasure in the field and the wedding feast teach that having found the kingdom, one has to give up everything one has, even his own spirit, in order to have a part in it. Having surrendered his own spirit, man no longer acts out of the spirit of self-will but by the will of God. His thoughts are no longer inspired by the spirit of self-interest but by God's self-abnegating spirit.

> **Rom 8:9** But ye are not in the flesh, but in the Spirit, if so be that the Spirit of God dwell in you. Now if any man have not the Spirit of Christ, he is none of his.

The 'faith' of a man that is part of God's kingdom is not at all the same as what is considered faith in the realm of man. It is not an exercise of one's mind in choosing to believe or have trust, hope and confidence in religion or God. Instead, like the faith of Jesus, it becomes an unbreakable and complete dependence on God: the sovereign and sole benefactor of the citizens of His kingdom. Works are no longer self-interested actions performed to avoid hell or prove ones' fitness for heaven, but are simply the evidence that the spirit of God, rather than the natural spirit of man, resides in the soul. This is what it means to "bring forth fruit meet for repentance" (**Mat 3:8**). The means of being part of the kingdom of heaven, is clear:

> **Matt 4:17** From that time Jesus began to preach, and to say, Repent: for the kingdom of heaven is at hand.

Repentance is a turning away not just from the mistakes you are ashamed of, but from every aspect of your natural psyche, your inner self. That is, turning away from the unclean spirit of man that is within you. It also involves a turning away from the realm of man, or as the apostle says "repentance from dead works" (**Heb 6:1**) to seek the spirit of God by faith. It is how one becomes a partaker of the divine nature (**2 Pet 1:4**). It is the process of progressively disentangling yourself from your own spirit, thoughts and actions and becoming filled with the spirit of God along with his thoughts and actions.

Citizenship in the kingdom of God is not irrevocable: one remains free to exit it at will. Just as the Holy Spirit is always calling sinners to repentance, the unclean spirit of man is always trying to regain control over the soul it has lost. The only points at which one can no longer choose is when one is no longer susceptible to the influence of the Holy Spirit by having committed the unpardonable sin, or at the other extreme, when one is sealed by the Holy Spirit and is no more susceptible to the unclean spirit of man. Citizens of God's kingdom are called to battle against the old spirit until it can no longer have any influence over them.

Are You Saved?

The Gospel

Many people become Christians because they want to avoid hellfire and have eternal bliss as the book of Romans puts it "to be saved from [God's] wrath" against unbelievers and workers of iniquity. Or as Jesus declared

> **John 3:16** For God so loved the world, that he gave his only begotten Son, that whosoever believeth in him should not perish, but have everlasting life.

Jesus' statement gives rise to some basic questions. If God is so loving can't He just save everyone instead of only those who believe? Why could God not just save everyone without sending Jesus to die for us? The answer to these questions is that even though God is all powerful, there are some limitations to God's power.

First God is limited by His own law **(Rom 8:2)** which declares that the wages of sin, is death **(1 Joh 3:4, Rom 6:23; Eze 18:20)**, and without the shedding of blood there is no remission of sin **(Heb 9:22)**. Accordingly, the only way to save man without breaking His own law and perishing Himself was to become a ransom for man **(Math 20:28)**.

Secondly, Jesus came not just to die for us but to make us free, not just from the penalty of sin, but from the bondage of sin **(Luke 4:18; Gal 5:1,13; 2Cor 3:17)**. Freedom cannot be forced; it requires individuals to make their own choices. By giving us knowledge of the gospel truth **(John 18:37)** God enables us to intelligently and freely choose His salvation or not **(John 8:32; Josh 24:15; 1 Ki 18:21)**, by means of our exercise of repentance and faith.

Is Belief Sufficient for Salvation?

Jesus does not propose to save anyone who does not really want to be saved. It is possible to want something as long as it does not cost you anything. In this case you don't really want it. This is true of the rich young ruler **(Luke 18:18, 23)** who wanted to inherit eternal life but wasn't prepared to give anything up for it. He had faith of sorts but it was not saving faith because he was half-hearted **(1 Joh 3:18)**.

Jesus made it clear that no man can serve two masters **(Mat 6:24.22-23)**. God does not reward the double-minded **(Jam 1:7-8)**. You cannot have this world and heaven also (Jam 4:4; 1 Joh 2:15-17). Only those who seek salvation more than anything else in this world will find it (Mat 13:45-46). There are many who profess to have faith yet do not have saving faith.

Just as God cannot save those who do not have saving faith, He also cannot save those who continue practicing sin, because sin is rebellion, not only against the law of God, but against the holiness of God himself in whom is no sin. After all, Jesus came not just to pay the penalty for our sin, but that we should no longer continue to sin (Joh 8:11; 1 Pe 4:1-2):

> **1 John 3:5** And ye know that he was manifested to take away our sins; and in him is no sin.
>
> **Heb 10:26** For if we sin wilfully after that we have received the knowledge of the truth, there remaineth no more sacrifice for sins,
>
> **2Pet 2:20** For if after they have escaped the pollutions of the world through the knowledge of the Lord and Saviour Jesus Christ, they are again entangled therein, and overcome, the latter end is worse... than the beginning.
>
> **Heb 6:4-6** For it is impossible for those who were once enlightened, and have tasted of the heavenly gift, and were made partakers of the Holy Ghost, And have tasted the good word of God, and the powers of the world to come, If they shall fall away, to renew them again unto repentance; seeing they crucify to themselves the Son of God afresh, and put him to an open shame.

This is why Jesus came not only to die as a ransom, making a way for the salvation of man (Luk 19:10), but to call sinners to repentance (Luke 5:32). Since, according to Scripture it is not enough to believe in Christ's sacrifice on behalf of man but faith must be combined with repentance (Mark 1:14-15).

> **2Pet 3:9** The Lord is ... not willing that any should perish, but that all should come to repentance.

Repentance is not just about wanting to avoid the punishment for sin (our moral failings) but wanting to avoid sin itself. Those who want to avoid the punishment of their sin, and feel remorse over its possible consequences, but not the sin that brings it, are just like Balaam, Esau and Judas. There are many Christians today who also selfishly want to avoid hell and go to heaven, but do not have real repentance. Can those who are selfish, which is in its very essence unchristian (2 Cor 5:15) go to heaven when the tenth commandment says "thou shalt not covet"?

A few verses before Jesus said that whosoever believes in him shall not perish but have everlasting life, He explained that only those who are born again (John 3:3), that is, who have died to their selfishness and sin (Rom 6:2,6-7) and been resurrected to new life, (Gal 2:20) will enter heaven.

Saved from Sin

Now if we have repentance and it is true that "with God all things are possible" (Mat 19:26) and "If ye have faith ... nothing shall be impossible unto you." (Matt 17:20) then God is not only able to save us from the consequences of sin, (eternal death and hell) but from continuing in sin. In fact, He can only make us free from the penalty of sin by making us free from doing acts of sin which is another reason why Jesus came down from heaven:

> **Matt 1:21** and thou shalt call his name JESUS: for he shall save his people from their sins.
>
> **Rom 8:3-4, 2** God sending his own Son in the likeness of sinful flesh ... condemned sin in the flesh: That the righteousness of the law might be fulfilled in us ... For the law of the Spirit of life in Christ Jesus hath made me free from the law of sin and death.
>
> **Rom 6:22** But now being made free from sin, and become servants to God, ye have your fruit unto holiness, and the end everlasting life.
>
> **1Pet 2:21-22** For even hereunto were ye called: because Christ also suffered for us, leaving us an example, that ye should follow his steps: Who did no sin, neither was guile found in his mouth:
>
> **1John 3:6-8** Whosoever abideth in him sinneth not: whosoever sinneth hath not seen him, neither known him... He that committeth sin is of the devil; ... For this purpose the Son of God was manifested, that he might destroy the works of the devil.

Why would God chose only to save us from the wages of sin, but not the sin itself if He is able to do so? A God that cannot or will not stop the murderer from murdering, the adulterer from adultery, the thief from stealing, the blasphemer from blaspheming, the proud from their pride or the covetous from their covetousness is no better than a pagan idol. The scriptures make it clear that Christ is able to keep us from falling into sin by making a way of escape for us, so that there no excuse for practising sin.

> **Jude 1:24** Now unto him that is able to keep you from falling, and to present you faultless

1 Cor10:13 God is faithful, who will not suffer you to be tempted above that ye are able; but will with the temptation also make a way to escape, that ye may be able to bear it.

This is why the Bible tells us no one will enter heaven while practising sin. Practical holiness is required to enter heaven (see also 1 Cor 6:9, Heb 12:14; Rev 3:21)

Ps 24:3-4 Who shall ascend into the hill of the LORD? or who shall stand in his holy place? He that hath clean hands, and a pure heart; who hath not lifted up his soul unto vanity, nor sworn deceitfully.

Ps 15:1-4 who shall abide in thy tabernacle? who shall dwell in thy holy hill? He that walketh uprightly, and worketh righteousness, and speaketh the truth in his heart. He that backbiteth not with his tongue, nor does evil to his neighbour, nor takes up a reproach against his neighbour. In whose eyes a vile person is contemned; but he honours them that fear the LORD. He that swears to his own hurt, and changeth not.

Isa 33:14-15 ...He that walketh righteously, and speaketh uprightly; he that despises the gain of oppressions, that shaketh his hands from holding of bribes, that stops his ears from hearing of blood, and shuts his eyes from seeing evil;

Now many argue that we don't have to overcome sin in practice, because faith is counted for righteousness. Jesus said "you shall know them by their fruits" (Matt 7:16-20; 12:33) and that everyone will in the last day be judged not by his claim of having faith but by his works (Mat 16:27; Rev 2:23; 20:12). Unless faith results in practical holiness, it is not saving faith but is dead (Jam 2:14, 17, 20, 26). This is not talking about doing good works to balance out your sin and prove you have faith, but about separating from sin.

Saved from Ourselves

Now this presents us with a problem: since the heart of man "is deceitful above all things and desperately wicked," (Jer 17:9) temptation and sin arises from with oneself (Jam 1:14-15), hence it is just as easy for a sinner to overcome sin as it is for a leopard to change its spots (Jer 13:23). The apostle Paul declared that even when he wanted to do right he could not, but instead on his own did the evil he did not want to do, because in his flesh was the law of sin. (Rom 7:14-24).

Clearly, no one can be saved from committing sin, unless he is first saved from himself, from his own selfishness, from his pride, from his own desires. Paul goes on to explain that Jesus in fact came to save man from himself, so that he need no longer be a slave to the desires of his own flesh, but be freed from its bondage (Rom 8:1-14; Gal 5:16). This is the purpose of the new birth, to give man a new heart: a new mind and a new spirit, free from the corruption of the flesh. Jesus came to save man from "all iniquity" and sin, so as to be enabled to do what is good and right and be truly holy (Tit 2:14; Eph 2:10; 4:24) "That the righteousness of the law might be fulfilled in us" (Rom 8:4), not in the afterlife but in the present. If Jesus does not have the power to save man from his own depravity now, He has no power to save man from the consequences of sin later.

The reason why so many professed believers are unable to overcome their sin, is not because God is unable or unwilling to give them power to do so, but because their repentance is a repentance that needs to repented of (2 Cor 7:10). It is superficial, it does not go deep enough. They repent from the symptoms of sin, but not the sin itself. They repent from the sin that their own desire conceives, but not from the source of those desires. Likewise their faith is also superficial, bordering on presumption.

Some think that being saved is a matter of something that took place the past (consequences or stain of sin) or will take place in the future (power and/or presence from sin). The reality is that salvation is only a matter of the continual present. You are either saved now from every aspect of sin or not saved at all. What happened in the past is of no consequence unless it continues in the present. At the end of life's journey no one will be asked if they were saved at some point, or hope to be saved in the next life, but if they are saved in that moment. The only salvation that operates in the moment in this life, is the salvation from our own inherent depravity, and being saved from that we are saved from sin and its consequences.

The Grace of God

Grace is Charity

The grace of God is a key concept in the Bible. It is the only means for the salvation of man. Without it no man can be saved, so it is vitally important to understand what it is and how it works. Now the Greek word translated as 'grace' in the New Testament is the root word from which we get the English word charity. In the Old Testament the root of the word that is translated as grace means "to bend or to stoop to bestow a favour to an inferior" which conveys the same idea. God's grace is simply his charity towards sinners.

Now charity is of no value unless the intended beneficiary accepts it. Some promote the idea that you have no choice in the matter: that God's grace is irresistible and cannot be frustrated or forfeited. Forcing charity on someone that does not want it is just tyranny. Heaven would be hell to those who do not want to be there. Instead, the Bible implores us not to receive God's grace, his charity towards us, in vain but to choose to serve God (e.g. Josh 24:15 and 1 Kings 18:21) and

> 2Cor 6:1 We... beseech you also that ye receive not the grace of God in vain.

An End or a Means?

Is charity an end in itself or just the means to an end? There is a proverb that says "Give a man a fish and you feed him for a day. Teach a man to fish and you feed him for a lifetime." This means that true charity does not satisfy a beggar's immediate want leaving him a beggar but enables him to overcome his condition to want no more. If the beggar represents a helpless sinner, and grace is God's charity, does God give us a fish or does He teach us to fish, or does He instead just give us a lifetime supply of fish?

Let us try to understand what God's charity, by defining grace in terms of these three alternatives: (1) Giving a beggar a guaranteed lifetime supply of fish so that he never has to beg again is like giving a sinner an unconditional pass to heaven. (2) Giving a beggar a single fish every time he begs is like giving a sinner a provisional pass to heaven; he won't starve to death as long as he keeps begging. (3) Lastly teaching the beggar how to fish is like transforming him into a new man, one who is fit to enter heaven.

The Grace of God

Most people would agree that solving the underlying reason for the beggars hunger is better than just giving him handouts. In the previous chapter we considered the object of God's charity. God does not propose to save man just from the consequences of his sin, nor just from committing acts of sin. Instead God seeks to save man from what excludes him from heaven, his own depravity, which is the source of man's sin; his selfishness, pride, vanity, etc. This is why salvation is not obtained by the keeping of the law, but by becoming a new creature. (Gal 6:15; Jn 3:3). In this context let us analyse each of these three alternatives.

In the first case, grace is considered to be an unconditional pass to enter heaven. This pass is "unmerited favour" because anyone, who at some point in their life accepts it, will be there no matter the evil of their lives, unless they decide they no longer want it. This kind of charity does not resolve the underlying issue of sin that puts us in need of grace to begin with. Having in this way entered heaven, the sinner cannot help but keep sinning for all eternity, unless he is somehow forced not to do so against his inclination. In this case heaven becomes either a jail for sinners or a home for automatons.

In the second case the beggar is given a slice of bread, so that he soon becomes hungry and needs to beg again. To avoid dying of hunger he must enrol in a welfare program and remain enrolled as a welfare recipient. In terms of grace, this is like a sinner being provisionally guaranteed entry into heaven as long as he continues to meet certain conditions. This could be believing some dogma, partaking of some sacrament or ritual, practicing devotion, or being enrolled in a church. Since one must accept these conditions to continue to be eligible for heaven, this charity is not unmerited, because continued charity is merited by the acceptance of the condition(s).

In terms of resolving the underlying issue of sin, this case is no different than the first. Having finally attained heaven, the sinner cannot but keep sinning. The sinfulness of the sinner is the same only that he has to jump more hurdles to get there. Is this more favourable than the first case? Additionally, if someone can feed a beggar for his entire life but keeps them begging by only giving him a slice of bread at a time, is it charity or an insult?

The final case, represents true charity. Grace is not any kind of welfare entitlement, but rather the means for transforming the beggar into a new man by resolving his underlying problem. God's grace is an instrument for accomplishing this transformation, which correctly used, enables the sinner to overcome not just sin but his own depravity and having done so, to become fit to enter heaven as a free agent, as Jesus said:

> **Rev 3:21** To him that overcometh will I grant to sit with me in my throne, even as I also overcame, and am set down with my Father in his throne.

Merited or Unmerited Favour?

The Jews in Jesus day were indisputably in possession of the unmerited favour or grace of God; they were His chosen people that had been entrusted with the oracles of God **(Rom 3:2)** and yet they were destroyed. Jesus explained to them that although they enjoyed the favour of God, this did not guarantee them a part in his kingdom. Paul says that God broke them off because of their blindness **(Rom 11:25)** and grafted the gentiles in their place. God's grace is certainly not an unmerited favour that entitles one an unconditional pass to heaven.

Is grace then God's unmerited favour that grants us a provisional entitlement to heaven, contingent on fulfilling certain conditions? For example, did not Jesus say that one must believe and be baptised to be saved?

> **Mark 16:16** He that believeth and is baptized shall be saved; but he that believeth not shall be damned.

If belief and baptism are the conditions for salvation, why were Simon the sorcerer **(Acts 8:13)** as well as Ananias and Sapphira **(Acts 5:1-9)** not saved? Jesus said that many even of those who believe and are baptised, who trust and hope in God's charity towards sinners, will not enter heaven. He told the parables of: the five foolish virgins, who were waiting for the coming of the bridegroom **(Mat 25:1-12)**; the man who travelled to the wedding feast hoping to enter **(Mat 22:1-13)**; and the many who have preached in his name and done many wonderful works who cry out "Lord, Lord" hoping to enter the kingdom of heaven **(Mat 7:21-23)**; to teach that many who believe they have met the conditions to enter heaven will be turned away. There is no work or group membership- **(John 8:39, Luke 3:8)** that merits an entitlement to heaven:

> **Rom 11:6** And if by grace, then is it no more of works: otherwise grace is no more grace. But if it be of works, then is it no more grace.

So grace is not any kind of unmerited favour that grants one a provisional entitlement to heaven.

The Grace of God

Past, Present or Future?

Those who think grace is an entitlement they received in the past to a future reward rely on modern bible translations of

> **Eph 2:8** For by grace are ye saved through faith; and that not of yourselves: it is the gift of God

These translate the original Greek phrase "χαριτι εστε σεσωσμενοι" (charis este sesosmenoi) in the past tense as "by grace you have been saved". They completely ignore that the tense of the operative word 'este' is present indicative active, which means that the operation of grace is a work of the present, not a work of the past nor a work of the future. The word 'sesosmenoi' (saved) is a perfect participle which means that it is a verb that is being used as an adjective, (in English we often add the suffix "-ing" to a verb to accomplish the same). This means that the word translated as 'saved', is more properly translated as 'saving'. This verse simply says "by faith you have saving grace now" it says nothing about having received any kind of entitlement to heaven in the past nor what will happen in the future.

If grace is the work of the present, it is ongoing, not in the sense of an ongoing reaffirmation of a past entitlement for some future benefit, but in the sense that both the entitlement and the benefit are in the present. What kind of salvation does grace grant us in the present? It can only be salvation from our present infirmity. Not salvation from past or future sin, nor from destruction, but salvation from the "the law of sin that is in my members", the "law, that, when I would do good, evil is present with me." (Rom 7:23, 21) From the lusts of the flesh that cause us to sin (Jam 1:14-15) that "lusteth against the Spirit, and the Spirit against the flesh: and these are contrary the one to the other: so that ye cannot do the things that ye would." (Gal 5:17) Grace is the instrument by which we can be saved from ourselves in the present.

Is it possible for grace to be a combination of these different alternatives? Does one first obtain a provisional pass to heaven, under which if some criteria are met such as keeping the law or doing good works, it becomes unconditional in the future? In other words, is salvation partly merited and partly unmerited? It does not matter how this merit is obtained, whether it is the result of a knowledge of and belief in God or some deed, if salvation is merited in any way, then it is not of grace, and if it is not of grace, it is not of

God but of man, who believes himself saved by virtue of the merit he has gained. He is like the Pharisee who thanked God for the virtue he believed that his faith had obtained for him, but all his supposed virtue did not result in him finding the grace he presumed he deserved (Luke 18:10-12).

Applied Grace

The instrument of grace on its own cannot save us any more than a tool can perform anything on its own: The instrument must be correctly used to be effective. What is the instrument of grace? There are two: faith and repentance (2 Pet 3:9; 2 Cor 7:10; Luke 13:3). Both faith (Rom 12:3; Eph 2:8) and repentance (Acts 5:31) are God's charitable gifts to us. We can only be saved from the present lusts of our flesh by continually exercising both faith and repentance. This is how it is "by grace that you are saved through faith."

The thing about grace is that, while God freely grants it to all men, not all have it in equal measure, and we are commanded to grow in grace (2 Pet 3:18). It is hard to see how one can grow an entitlement to heaven, but we can grow in repentance and faith. "He giveth more grace" to those who ask and make correct use of it. "Wherefore he saith, God resisteth the proud, but giveth grace unto the humble" (Jas 4:6). That is, He gives grace to those who are "of a contrite and humble spirit" (Isa 57:15). God increases the faith (2 Cor 1:3) of those who ask and earnestly seek Him (Luk 17:5-6; Mat 7:7-8).

God's grace is not some kind of entitlement that He gives us because He is partial towards us, out of favouritism because we please Him somehow. It is the charity that He gives out of pity to all who are perishing. His gifts of repentance and faith are unmerited and free but having received them is of no value unless we make correct use of them. They are a spiritual life buoy, instruments by which we can overcome our flesh and walk in His Spirit, and doing so, overcome sin in this life and continue to do so until we overcome death (Jam 1:15) and enter eternal life. There is no concept in the Bible of past grace granting us any future reward. Grace only operates in the continual present. A life buoy will not save a drowning man unless he continues clinging to it with all his might.

Let us not frustrate or fall short of the grace of God (Gal 2:21; Heb 12:15) by thinking that it, either conditionally or unconditionally grants sinners an entitlement to heaven. Only saints will enter heaven (1 Jn 3:6-9; Jn 3:3). Instead the application of God's grace transforms sinners into saints, exhibiting righteousness and true holiness. (Eph 4:22-24)

Let us not frustrate the grace of God by thinking that there is some belief, devotion, or work that sinners must do to obtain or retain God's grace. For "while we were yet enemies we were reconciled to God by the death of His son." (Rom 5:8, 10; 1 Pet 3:18; Micah 7:19-19)

Let us also not frustrate the grace of God by thinking that having received God's grace, our own efforts, beyond the means of grace, have any merit in obtaining heaven, "For to him that worketh is the reward not reckoned of grace, but of debt." (Rom 4:4). God's grace is sufficient to save all those who make correct use of the gifts of God's grace (Tit 3:7). We cannot do that unless we first rediscover and exercise true faith and true repentance.

True Godliness

A Form of Godliness

Some years ago, the motif "What Would Jesus Do", was popular among young conservative Evangelicals. This imitation of Christ in decision making was a small but positive step towards the practical godliness that Christians are called to follow (1 Tim 6:11). In contrast we are warned that in the last days many will have an empty form of godliness, and many will be deceived by this superficial religion (2Tim 3:1, 5; Jam 1:26). They think their salvation is sure because of their belief in God, their devotions, their "relationship" with God or their lifestyle, but their religion is just an empty form: an appearance of godliness. They are "whited sepulchres" who look good on the outside while being lovers of themselves, covetous, proud, unholy, high-minded, lovers of pleasures more than lovers of God (2 Tim 3:2).

Many believe themselves saved because of Christ's death on the cross but man is not saved by Christ's death, but by his life (Rom 5:10). Christ's death was only the means by which Christ obtained the legal right to begin the work of restoring in man the image of God without which no one can see God (Col 3:10; Eph 4:24; Heb 12:14). The right to become the author of salvation (Heb 5:9; 2:10) and the architect of godliness. It was not in Christ's death, but in His life that the power of God to restore man is revealed (Acts 10:38; Luk 4:32). Unless Christ lives His life in us (Col 1:27; Rom 8:9; Mat 28:18) our religion will be an empty form of Godliness (2 Cor 13:5) that denies the power thereof. Those in whom Christ dwells will walk as he walked (1 Joh 2:6), not in external words and works but, in their innermost being, they will reflect Christ. Their hearts will beat in time with His heart, His thoughts will be their thoughts, His feelings will be their feelings, and His choices will be their choices. Put simply, they will have the mind of Christ (1 Cor 2:16; Phil 2:5, 8).

The Life of Christ

No one can share the life of Christ, or in the power of His resurrection, unless they have first shared in the likeness of his death (Rom 6:3; Phil 3:10; Rom 6:4-7; Gal 5:24). What was the likeness of his death? It was not a metaphorical death, not a death of incredulity, it was not about the abandonment of a few lusts, or of some deeply held opinions, but the giving up of everything that made Him who He was. It was less so the death of His body than of His spirit, His psyche, (spirit in the sense of **Mat 5:3; Matt 26:41; Jo 11:33; Acts 17:16; 18:25; Rom 1:9; 1 Cor 5:5; Eph 4:23; 1 Pet 3:4**) because "it is the spirit that quickeneth, the flesh profiteth nothing" (**John 6:63**). Unless we share in the likeness of His death and our spirit (**1 Cor 2:11**), is crucified with Christ (**Gal 2:20**), the Spirit of Christ cannot dwell in us, and all our religion is in vain.

Now Christ was "the Lamb slain from the foundation of the world" (**Rev 13:8**) not because He pessimistically looked forward to His death one day outside the walls of Jerusalem, but because, from that very moment, He began to suffer the penalty for sin which was: "in the day that thou eatest thereof thou shalt surely die" (**Gen 2:17**). The original Hebrew puts it as, "dying ye shall die." As soon as Christ chose to become the ransom for man, He began to die to who He was. He chose to give up the very attributes of God; his omnipresence, omnipotence, His divine power, and majesty and become a man; a vile worm (**Rom 8:3; Heb 2:6; Ps 22:6**). He chose to take upon himself sinful, human nature which is contrary to the immaculate holiness of God (**Rom 1:3; Gal 5:17; Jer 17:9; Rom 7:18; 2 Joh 1:7**).

It is from the corruption within our own flesh that our temptations arise (**Jam 1:13-14**), not from without. Being made in the likeness of sinful flesh, Christ had to struggle like we do against his own flesh. The scripture says He was touched with the feelings of our weaknesses (**Heb 4:15**) which is not just feelings of being tired or hungry, but the peculiar infirmities of sinful flesh: love of pleasure, self-confidence, pride, selfishness etc. This is why:

> **Heb 2:18** [having] suffered being tempted, he is able to succour them that are tempted.

Christ took no pleasure in the weak, corrupt, sinful flesh He was to take upon Himself. His infinite perfection and holiness recoiled from the horrific thought. As a man, Christ had no confidence in Himself (**Phil 3:3**). This is why He could not trust His own will (**Joh 6:38**), He had no strength in His flesh to do God's will (**Joh 5:30**), and He could not trust Himself to speak His own words (**Joh 14:10**). There is no way Jesus could have been pleased with Himself, or self-satisfied or proud in any way. Looking back to the perfection, holiness, glory, power, and wisdom that had been His in the courts of heaven, how could He do anything but abhor himself and long to be restored to the pure atmosphere of heaven? This is the mind of Christ and the mind of those to whom Christ has been revealed. Their eyes have been opened to the glory of God, they have seen the perfection of beauty and long to be restored into the image of God.

Self-Abhorrence

This is the same experience in Job's case. We read "I have heard of thee by the hearing of the ear; but now mine eye seeth thee: wherefore I abhor myself, and repent in dust and ashes." (Job 42:1-6). No one can catch a glimpse of the glory and purity of Jesus Christ without abhorring himself. This is not simply a one-time experience that comes at conversion but every time that one sees the unveiled Christ. He who does not abhor himself has not seen Jesus and cannot understand the meaning of redemption. No one can die to self, no man can share in the likeness of Christ's death, unless he first abhors himself. He must first realise the corruption, the deceitfulness, of self and hate it so much as to continually desire to be free from himself (Joh 12:25; Luk 14:26). You see this is the secret of true repentance which all must have who will be found worthy of salvation. Repenting from themselves, they, like Christ, earnestly and continually cry out to be saved from themselves: "not my own will but thine be done" (Luk 22:42).

> **Heb 5:7** Who in the days of his flesh, when he had offered up prayers and supplications with strong crying and tears unto him that was able to save him from death, and was heard in that he feared.

This verse makes no sense if we believe it says that Jesus wanted to be saved from dying and that He was heard because of his prayers, because He did die on the cross. This verse only makes sense if we realise that the word translated as 'from' where it says, "saved from death" can also be translated, and is translated many times in the Bible, as the word 'by'. The verse can then be read as "unto him that was able to save him by the means of death and was heard in that he feared." This is saying that Christ wanted to be saved from eternal death, and the only way he could be saved from it was by the means of death to himself: to his own will. His prayer was heard, and as He continually died to self, the Father continually dwelt in Him. Only then could the life of God, God's will, God's words, God's work, God's Spirit, God's power, be manifest in and through Christ (Joh 14:10). Only as we continually plead to be saved from self - to die to self - can God continually dwell in us. Only as we share in His life of continual death to self can we share in the likeness of his death and do the works of Christ (John 14:12). As Paul says:

> 2Cor 4:10 Always bearing about in the body the dying of the Lord Jesus, that the life also of Jesus might be made manifest in our body.

Take Up His Cross

This is what Jesus meant when he declared "take up your cross daily and follow me" (Luk 9:23). It was not to struggle against a wooden cross one Friday afternoon, but to struggle against the cross of our corrupt human nature (our own psyche, or spirit) for as long as we live. Dying ye shall die: a daily dying to oneself. This is the likeness of His death which we must share if we are to share in the likeness of His resurrection because, as the scripture says:

> John 12:24 Except a corn of wheat fall into the ground and die, it abideth alone: but if it die, it bringeth forth much fruit.

It is only as we understand the likeness of Christ's death, the nature of his suffering, that we see the glory of the Lord. Then as we put on the mind of Christ and share in His suffering, we are changed into His glorious image (1 Pet 4:1; 2 Cor 3:18). Christ invites us to take His yoke on ourselves (Mat 11:29), to follow His example (1 Pet 2:21), to overcome as He overcame (Rev 3:21). How did He overcome? Watch Him in the garden of Gethsemane dying to self, gaining the victory by pleading with God with strong crying and tears. Jesus invites us today to join Him in His passion; to die to self together with Him. He said:

> Matt 26:38-39 My soul is exceeding sorrowful, even unto death: tarry ye here, and watch with me. And he went a little further, and fell on his face, and prayed, saying, O my Father... not as I will, but as thou [wilt].

But even Christ's closest disciples could not understand Christ. Their own self-love had blinded them to the most essential truths about salvation and their desperate need. They had no sense of the need to be saved from themselves. They believed Christ had come to save them, not from self, but in self. It was a hard lesson for the apostle Peter to learn. Only after he denied Christ did he realise who he really was, and his self-deception was unmasked. Follow him as, in self-abhorrence, he makes his anguished way back to Gethsemane, hear his bitter cry, watch him in indescribable sorrow of soul fall, broken, weeping on the rock, no more the ambitious, self-confident disciple, no more sure of himself, no more blind to the depravity of his own heart. A broken spirit, a contrite heart - thou oh lord will not despise (Ps 51:17). -

Understanding Christianity

Finally, he understood repentance: self must die that Christ may live. Peter now had the mind of Christ. He could now share in the likeness of His death and overcome even as Christ overcame. Christ could be reborn in his heart and live His life in him. He was now ready to take up his cross and share in Christ's glory.

For too long Christ has been standing without the door, waiting to come in, but there is no room in men's hearts: they are full of self. Many are content with a theory of Christianity, a veneer of supposed faith, a superficial religion that claims salvation, not from self, but in self. They do not desire the mind of Christ. They want a form of godliness that in this life denies the power of God to recreate man in his own image. They look for a wide gate and a broad way, one that is wide enough for the flesh to enter, where self does not need to be left behind.

> **Matt 7:13-14** Enter ye in at the strait gate: for wide [is] the gate, and broad [is] the way, that leadeth to destruction, and many there be which go in thereat: Because strait [is] the gate, and narrow [is] the way, which leadeth unto life, and few there be that find it.

Holiness

What is Holiness?

Holiness is a key attribute of God, one that He desires us to have in common with Him (1 Pet 1:15-16). But it is not just something God would like us to have, but something we must have, since "without holiness no man shall see God" (Heb 12:14). Saints, by definition, are holy because they are sanctified which means having been made holy. Unfortunately, many people misunderstand what it means to be holy, and others do not understand how one becomes holy.

The word holy is used in several diverse ways in the Bible, but it comes from a Hebrew root that means to be ceremonially or morally clean (2 Cor 7:1; 1 Thes 4:7). It is used interchangeably with words such as "undefiled" (Heb 7:26, 1 Cor 3:17), "without blame" (Eph 1:4; 1 Thes 3:13) "without spot or blemish" (Eph 5:27), "unreprovable" (Col 1:22), "just and good" (Rom 7:12) "free from sin" (Rom 6:18,22), and "righteousness" (Eph 4:24; Rev 22:11, Luke 1:75). By extension, holiness includes the idea of being separate from anything that defiles such as idols, infidels, or sinners (2 Cor 6:14-17; Heb 7:26). For example...

> 1Thess 4:7 For God hath not called us unto uncleanness, but unto holiness.

Now some people think that holiness is just a legal status that one obtains when one is converted so that one can be holy in theory while not being so in practice. This is contrary to texts in the Bible that say we are to be holy even as God is holy (1 Pet 1:15-16). God's holiness is most certainly not theoretical. Jesus commanded His followers to be perfect even as God is perfect (Matt 5:48) which includes being holy like God is holy, and the Bible encourages us to imitate Christ's holy behaviour (1 Pet 2:21-23) and to cleanse or purify ourselves even as He is pure and holy (1 Joh 3:2-3).

What Holiness Is Not

Now the Jews thought that keeping the letter of the law made them holy since being holy means to be free from sin, which they defined as the transgression of the law. There are two problems with this understanding: first sin is not just breaking the letter of the law but breaking the spirit of the law (Rom 2:29; 7:6, 14) and includes all our moral failings such as pride and selfishness. Secondly, the works of the law cannot make anyone holy (Gal 2:16;

3:2), since all have sinned and "whosoever shall offend in one point is guilty of all" (Jam 2:10). Furthermore, since it is as impossible for those accustomed to doing evil to do good as it is for a leopard to change its spots, (Jer 13:23) even the good things that we do and "all our righteousness's are as filthy rags" (Isa 64:6).

In contrast, many Christians who talk about faith alone want to believe that they can be holy even while violating the law of God because they take Colossians 2:14, which talks about 'the handwriting of ordinances" being blotted out, to mean not just the ceremonial ordinances about food and drink offerings and ritual washings, but the ten commandments as well (Col 2:14; Heb 9:1, 10). Having thus removed God's moral code, they replace it with charity, so they say that holiness is all about doing works of charity rather than the works of the law. They like to cite "let your light shine before men that they may see your good works and glorify your father which is in heaven" (Mat 5:16). If, as they claim, the law was abolished then it would be impossible for anyone to sin and accordingly, impossible for anyone to go to hell which is clearly not the case (1 Joh 2:1; Rom 7:7). "Do we then make void the law through faith? God forbid: yea, we establish the law." (Rom 3:31). Jesus himself declared that He did not come to destroy the law, and that it would stand until heaven and earth passed away (Mat 5:17-18). Even if the law was abolished, works of charity cannot make anyone holy for the same reason that the works of the law cannot.

The only real difference between those who claim holiness is found in doing works of some kind and those who say it is by faith alone is, not one of substance but, of degrees. Whether it consists of works of the body or of the mind, all have a checklist of what constitutes holiness. The Jewish checklist was extraordinarily long, having added to the law of God thousands of additional requirements. Others limit themselves to the seven Noahide laws. The checklist of many Christians has only two items: to love God supremely and your neighbour as yourself. Still others have only a single item on their list: belief in Jesus Christ as their personal saviour.

It does not matter whether your list is long or short, only that whatever it requires, it is the work of your own prerogative. As such, those who meet the requirements of their checklist think they are somehow holier than those who do not. They satisfy themselves in doing so, expecting to be entitled to certain advantages or blessings in continuing to do so.

The Test of Holiness

The scriptures repeatedly tell us that all will be judged by their works (Mat 16:27) to determine if they are holy, not just in words or in theory but, indeed and in truth. When Jesus said, "by their fruit ye shall know them," He continued by saying that many in the last day will point to all the good works they have done but they will not be counted (Mat 7:20-23). Instead, they are "like whited sepulchres, which indeed appear beautiful outward but within are full of... all uncleanness" (Mat 23:27). It is not the outside of the cup that should be made clean but the inside (Mat 23:25-26). Those that are holy are not known by the external works of the law (Gal 6:15), nor works of charity but by internal works of holiness. God does not look at the outside appearance but looks on the heart (1 Sam 16:7). He looks at the fruit of His grace on the heart as revealed in works of holiness. He does not look at the intentions of the heart. The road to hell is paved with good intentions as Uzzah found when he tried to stop the ark of the covenant from tipping (2 Sam 6:3-8) or as Nadab and Abihu found when they offered incense using strange fire before the Lord (Lev 10:1).

The fruit of God's grace upon the heart, the work of holiness, is not a work of your own prerogative. John the Baptist tells us it is the fruit of repentance (Mat 3:8) as revealed in works of repentance (Acts 26:20). This is the fruit that God waits for like a husbandman patiently waits for the precious fruit (Jas 5:7), not willing that any should perish (2 Pet 3:9).

The Bible places works of repentance in contrast to what it calls "dead works" or "works of the law." The essential difference between works of repentance and works of the law (or even charity) is that the latter are works that man does in his own strength and by his own will. Works of repentance, on the other hand, are impossible for man himself to do because they are contrary to the flesh, that is, our selfishness and pride. Only as man surrenders to God, can the works of repentance appear in man's heart. For this same reason penance is not the work of repentance, because it is not the work of God but of man. So, works of repentance are works that God does in and through man as God alone ordains.

> **Isa 26:12** LORD, thou wilt ordain peace for us: for thou also hast wrought all our works in us.
>
> **Phil 2:13** For it is God which worketh in you both to will and to do of [his] good pleasure.

Understanding Christianity

> **Phil 1:6** Being confident of this very thing, that he which hath begun a good work in you will perform [it] until the day of Jesus Christ:

The work of God is the work of bringing man to repentance (Acts 5:31), to break the spirit of man (Mat 21:44), to unmask the corruption of his soul and to humble him into the dust (1 Pet 5:6). It leads man to abhor himself and repent in dust and ashes (Job 42:6), that self may die (Rom 6:6) and a new man arise, "created in righteousness and true holiness" (Eph 4:24), in the image of Christ (Col 3:10). Only in repentance can man do the works of repentance, since they are the manifestation of a character transformed (Rom 12:2) by the grace of God.

Internal and External Holiness

Works of repentance are, by definition, holy works and include such things as self-distrust, self-denial, self-abasement, meekness, patience, long-suffering, gentleness, temperance, and purity. These "works" are the external evidence of internal holiness. They are works which can only proceed from holiness, and which the Lord will accept in the day when every man will be judged according to his works.

Holiness is not found in any work that we may do that is tainted by any selfishness or pride. Holiness is not found in any work that in any way glorifies self, whether in this life or the life to come. Holiness is only found in those things that glorify God alone. The essence of holiness is the removing of self out of the way that Christ may be revealed. It is the decrease of self that God may increase. Since this is the essence of repentance, the works of repentance can be non-other than holy.

Holiness is not keeping the letter of the law, but it is the fulfilling of the spirit of the law (Rom 7:6). Those who, according to the first great commandment, (Matt 22:37-38) love God above all things and put Him first before their own interests, cannot but separate themselves from all sin and iniquity (Heb 7:26; 1 Joh 2:1; Ps 51:2). They do not just seek pardon for their past misdeeds but seek to purify their present thoughts and actions from evil (1 John 1:9; Jam 4:8).

Those who are holy also seek to encourage others to be holy even as they are holy. They do this by reflecting God's long-suffering, mercy, and charity towards others, to bring them also to repentance. Yet while the fruit of holiness includes being merciful as well as avoiding sin, the Lord will not accept any work, charity, or work of the law in the place of works of repentance. Some may try to counterfeit holiness or works of repentance with works such as false humility or public self-denial for outward show, to deceive (2 Cor 11:13-15) for personal gain, but, like an insincere faith, these are of no value before God.

Obtaining Holiness?

Repentance, Holiness, or righteousness come only from Christ by faith (Acts 5:31, Gal 2:21; 3:21; Rom 8:3-4; Rom 9:30). That is, it comes from recognising our present need of it and earnestly seeking God for it (Heb 11:6). All those that sincerely do this will obtain it.

> 1Thes5:23-24 And the very God of peace sanctify you wholly; and I pray God your whole spirit and soul and body be preserved blameless unto the coming of our Lord Jesus Christ. Faithful is he that calleth you, who also will do it.

> 2Cor 7:1 Having therefore these promises, dearly beloved, let us cleanse ourselves from all filthiness of the flesh and spirit, perfecting holiness in the fear of God.

Those who feel no need for holiness or who do not strive for it will not obtain it and, no matter their faith, regardless of their keeping of the law or works of charity, will find like the man who turned up at the wedding feast without the wedding garment, (Matt 22:1-14) that their belief, hope, trust and effort to attend the wedding was insufficient to gain an entry.

> Matt 22:13-14 Then said the king to the servants, Bind him hand and foot, and take him away, and cast him into outer darkness; there shall be weeping and gnashing of teeth. For many are called, but few are chosen.

It is impossible for man to make himself holy, but God offers us not theoretical but practical holiness if we are seriously willing to obtain it. If we seek it with all our heart, and with our soul, and with all our mind, and with all our strength we will obtain it. And only those who do so will see God.

> 1 John 3:2 Beloved, now are we the sons of God, and it doth not yet appear what we shall be: but we know that, when he shall appear, we shall be like him; for we shall see him as he is.

God's Law

The Law of God or Moses?

There are many Christians who just don't know what to do about God's law. Some say it was abolished at the cross, others say that it is binding on the unconverted but not on Christians, or that Jesus fulfilled the law for us so that we are free from the claims of the law. Some say keeping the law is optional but has merit and others that it must be kept in order to be saved. This is compounded by confusion about the different bodies of law that are found in the Bible: civil laws, moral laws, ceremonial laws of rituals and health laws. These laws are not all the same.

Let's begin to unravel this issue by dividing the laws found in the Bible into two categories: the Law of God and the Law of Moses. The law of God was audibly spoken (Ex 20:1-2, 22, Deut 4:12-13) and directly written by God himself (Ex 31:18, Ex 32, 16), and the law of Moses was spoken (Ex 24:3) and written by Moses (Ex 24:4, Deut 31:9,24-26) under the inspiration of God. The law of God was written in stone (Ex 31:18, Deut 4:12-13) and stored inside the ark of the covenant (Deut 10:5) but the law of Moses was written in a book (Ex 24:4,7) and stored beside the ark of the covenant (Deut 31:26, 1 King 8:9). The law of God was given by Him to Moses (Ex 31:18) and applies to everyone (Ex 20:10), whereas the Law of Moses was given by him to the Levites (Deut 31:25) and applies only to the Jews (Ex 12:43-48). The Law of God deals with morals (Ex 20) and defines sin (Rom 7:7, 1 Joh 3:4), the Law of Moses deals with ceremonies, civil governance and health and defines offerings for sin (Lev 7:37). Keeping the Law of God brings blessings and liberty (Jam 1:25) but keeping the Law of Moses brings bondage (Gal 5:1-3). The nature of the Law of God is spiritual (Rom 7:12,14) but the nature of the Law of Moses is carnal (Heb 9:23; Heb 7:16).

There is no penalty for breaking the Law of Moses, but death is the penalty for breaking the Law of God (Rom 6:23, Ecc 12:13-14, Jam 2:12). Christ's death abolished the Law of Moses (Lev 7:37, Dan 9:26-27, Mat 27:51, Eph 2:15, Col 2:14-17, Heb 7:18) while establishing the Law of God through faith (Rom 3:31, Rom 2:13, Mat 5:17-19, Mat 19:16-19, Jam 2:10-12, Heb 8:10, John 14:15, 1 John 5:2-3, John 15:10, Rev 14:12, Rev 22:14-15). The apostle Paul made the distinction between the Law of God and the Law of Moses clear when he wrote:

God's Law

1 Cor 7:19 Circumcision is nothing, and uncircumcision is nothing, but the keeping of the commandments of God.

Civil Laws and Health Laws

While the Law of Moses is typically considered as being mostly ceremonial, it includes matters of health and civil governance which are not really ceremonial. The purpose of the ceremonial law was to point the Israelites forward to the future ministry and sacrifice of Christ (Heb 10:1; Heb 9:9-12) and, having been fulfilled, they no longer serve a purpose. However, this is not true of the civil and health laws.

The civil laws relate to property and inheritance (Duet 24:7), lending and interest (Exodus 22:25) treatment of foreigners, (Ex 22:21) crime and punishment, (Ex 21:12-36) the number and location of sanctuary cities in the land (Num 35:11-28; Josh 20:7-8), and the style of governance pertaining only to the nation of Israel. Their underlying principles remain valid, but the historic and cultural context they operated in no longer exists, so they cannot be practically implemented in the same way. It would be irresponsible to say that since Christ's death, crime no longer needs to punished, inheritances should not be respected and foreigners can be exploited.

The various health laws (Lev 13-14) deal with matters of personal hygiene (Lev 15:11), quarantine, diet (Lev 11) and avoiding sexually transmitted disease (Due 23:10-11; Lev 15:19). Again the underlying principles are valid but in some cases there are different methods available today for achieving the same outcome. Again it would be irresponsible to not quarantine those with deadly infectious diseases, to invite infection by disregarding hygiene, or to invite chronic disease by being careless about one's diet.

In summary, while the laws of Moses are not legally binding, the principles they are based on remain valid; the ceremonial laws help us understand God's plan of redemption and the health and civil laws help us maintain healthy societies and healthy physical bodies. The law of God however remains legally binding on all men. Imagine a land where murder, robbery and deception are permitted by law. To say that the law of God was transitory or applies only to the Jews is to ignore that every one of the Ten Commandments, except the fifth and ninth, is explicitly stated in the book of Genesis before the law was "given" to the Jews at Mt Sinai. All are also explicitly repeated or examples of them being kept are found in the New Testament.

Abolishing the Law

If God's law has been abolished then sin has also been abolished since where there is no law, there is no sin (Rom 4:15, 1 Joh 3:4, Rom 7:7). And if there is no sin, there is no more penalty for sin, and no need for a saviour from sin or its penalty. As soon as the law of God is invalid, there is no further need for Christ. If we minimise the law of God by reducing its scope or reach, we belittle Christ who came to deliver us from the curse of the law (Gal 3:13) and if we magnify God's law we magnify Christ.

Now we minimise the reach of God's law by saying it only applies to the Jews. We reduce the scope of the law by reading only the letter of the law, and ignoring the spirit of the law. Jesus came to teach the far reaching nature of God's law: that one can break the law while keeping the letter of the law. For example, committing adultery by just lusting after a woman (Mat 5:28), or being guilty of murder simply by being angry against another without cause (Mat 5:21-22). It is the desire of the heart, not just actions of the body that the law condemns. Guilt is not averted because of the lack of opportunity to carry out one's desires.

Others claim to keep the spirit of the law which is to love God above all things and their neighbour as themselves and feel free to ignore the letter of the law (Luk 10:27). For example, they may claim to keep the spirit of the sixth commandment, "thou shalt not commit adultery" (Ex 20:14) while committing serial polygamy (Mat 5:31-32). This is not keeping the spirit of the law but twisting the law to suit oneself. The spirit of the commandment is that a man or woman should be the faithful spouse of one wife or husband for their entire life. Others claim to keep the fourth commandment by observing any day of their own choosing. The spirit of this commandment is that the seventh day has been chosen by God as holy and man is to honour God by honouring His will. Changing the particulars of God's law to suit oneself does not magnify the law but makes it subordinate to our own desires, and doing so undermines Christ.

Magnifying the Law and Belittling Christ

It is, however, also possible to magnify the law of God in a way that belittles Christ. When we magnifying our own keeping of the law so as to reduce our need of Christ, we diminish our sin and reduce our need of a saviour. This contravenes the purpose of the law which is to open our eyes to our need of Christ (Gal 3:24) that we might be redeemed from sin and its penalty by Him (Rom 8:3-4). The law is our schoolmaster: it reveals our shortcomings like a mirror that reveals the dirt on our face. It is not, as many suppose, a "to do" list but a report card by which we can determine our failings and need of Christ. Its entire purpose is to bring us to repentance. That the Lord "is longsuffering… not willing that any should perish, but that all should come to repentance," (2 Pet 3:9) clearly reveals that the law is not restricted to a few but applies to all.

Those who presume to magnify the law of God by their own keeping of the law are not magnifying the law but themselves. To claim that one keeps the law, either in whole or in part, means that one has no sin, and is claiming to be righteous in whole or in part. In either case, it is a claim of moral superiority. The parable of the Pharisee and the publican (Luk 18:10-14) tells us that God does not listen to those who think they are morally superior, but to those who recognize their moral weakness. No matter how good we think we are, the Bible is clear that all are evil and "none is good but God"(Mat 19:17) because everyone is morally unclean, and all our righteouesnesses (or attempts to do right) are as a filthy rags (Isa 64:6) because no one can bring "a clean thing out of an unclean" (Job 14:5) and it is as impossible for man to do good as it is for a leopard to change its spots (Jer 13:23). It is accordingly impossible for anyone to claim moral superiority because of their attempts to keep the law, because he who offends in one point is guilty of all (Jam 2:10) and even if they were to keep the whole law, there is no righteousness to be found in the keeping of the law (Rom 3:21; 9:31, Gal 2:21; 3:21). Righteousness can only be obtained like the publican: in humbly seeking the grace of God.

Now some turn around and claim to magnify Christ, by being careless about the law, "that grace may abound" (Rom 6:1). They misunderstand grace and make a mockery of it, and in doing so do not magnify Christ but diminish both Him and the law together. God's grace is not some kind of free "get out of jail" card that permits one to treat sin lightly. It is the means by which He brings one to repentance. Repentance is a profound recognition and abhorrence of our moral weakness in light of the holiness of God's law and an earnest desire for holiness in the inward man. Repentance is not possible without a clear understanding of God's law that reveals to us our moral wretchedness. The broader the scope and reach of the law the greater our sense of wretchedness is and the greater our need of Christ. The greater our need of Christ's grace, the more we will love God as Jesus said "to whom little is forgiven, the same loveth little" (Luk 7:47) so the more forgiveness we need and receive, the more our love for God. This is why Jesus said "if ye love me keep my commandments" (John 15:10) and "This is the love of God that we keep his commandments" (1 John 5:3).

If we do not seek to keep God's commandments, not just in letter but in spirit, we will not see our inability to do so and we will not earnestly seek Christ for help so we will not receive help from Him and we will have but little love for Him. We cannot love the Lord our God with all our heart and mind and soul and strength unless we see our moral weakness in its fullness and with all our heart seek Him to obtain grace. This will only happen when we magnify the law of God and, understanding the extent of its scope and reach, in continual humble repentance fall at the feet of Jesus. Only then will Christ be magnified in our hearts and in the world as the saviour of mankind.

Forgiveness

A Means to an End

At the heart of the gospel is the forgiveness (or justification) made possible by Christ's death. Yet, notwithstanding its great cost, many people take it for granted. They talk about grace, by which, in part, they mean unconditional forgiveness. God's grace is certainly unconditional but, misunderstanding the operation of God's grace, they also misunderstand God's forgiveness. They misinterpret the text "we have... forgiveness according to the riches of His grace" (Eph 1:7) to claim that receiving God's grace means being forgiven, but the text only says that we can obtain forgiveness through God's grace.

God's grace is not an end in itself but the means to an end. As we discussed in the chapter "The Grace of God" the gifts of God's grace are free but they must be exercised in order to obtain any benefit from them. For example God has given to every man a measure of faith (Rom 12:3) but it must be exercised in order to be saved (Eph 2:8). Similarly repentance is a free gift of God's grace (Acts 5:31; 2 Tim 2:25) but we must choose to exercise repentance in order to obtain God's forgiveness. Put simply, forgiveness can only be obtained using the currency of repentance. There is no such thing as unconditional forgiveness in the Bible, because God does not forgive the unrepentant.

> **Luke 17:3** Take heed to yourselves: If thy brother trespass against thee, rebuke him; and if he repent, forgive him.
>
> **Acts 8:22** Repent therefore of this thy wickedness, and pray God, if perhaps the thought of thine heart may be forgiven thee.
>
> **Acts 2:38** Then Peter said unto them, Repent, and be baptized every one of you in the name of Jesus Christ for the remission of sins,
>
> **Acts 3:19** Repent ye therefore, and be converted, that your sins may be blotted out;
>
> **Luke 13:3** I tell you, Nay: but, except ye repent, ye shall all likewise perish.
>
> **2Pet 3:9** The Lord is not slack concerning his promise, as some men count slackness; but is longsuffering to us-ward, not willing that any should perish, but that all should come to repentance.

Understanding Christianity

What about love?

Confusing love with forgiveness, some will argue that Jesus said we are to love our enemies. They interpret this to mean we must forgive the unrepentant. The Bible tells us we are to love our enemies in the same way that God loves sinners. God extends His grace to everyone and has a spirit of compassion towards them; He does not cherish any grievances against those who hate Him nor withhold that which is good for them. God requires us to do likewise:

> **Matt 5:44-45** ...Love your enemies, bless them that curse you, do good to them that hate you, and pray for them which despitefully use you, and persecute you; That ye may be the children of your Father which is in heaven: for he maketh his sun to rise on the evil and on the good, and sendeth rain on the just and on the unjust.

Since God can only forgive the repentant, the entire object of God's love, grace and goodness is to lead men to repentance **(Rom 2:4)**, that they might be forgiven. Those who claim to be followers of Christ ought to do the same for the very same reason. Loving the sinner has nothing to do with carrying on as if sin does not matter, but on eliminating sin. To forgive those who do not want to abandon their sins defeats God's plan to redeem man from sin.

It is not surprising that today's humanistic Christianity has reframed what forgiveness is about, The 1828 edition of Webster's dictionary entry on forgiveness says *"The original and proper phrase is to forgive the offense, to send it away, to reject it, that is, not to impute it, [put it to] the offender."* The modern definition of 'forgive' is *"to cease to feel resentment against (an offender)"*. The critical focus today is no longer on the offence and its consequences, much less the offender, but on the offended or victim. It is now all about how the victim feels. The implied suggestion that God selfishly forgives for the sake of His feelings, is beyond absurd.

When God forgives, He does not change His feelings towards the sinner, He takes away the sin. Satan, however, wants to keep the sin but change our feelings towards it. Also by confusing us about what it means to forgive, guilt can be shifted from the offender to the offended. Thus the victim of crime who tries to defend himself is charged with assault and battery and those that try to protect the innocent from predators are guilty of hate crimes. In today's view, God is unjust for expelling Lucifer from heaven and depriving him of his angelic rights in order to protect the happiness of heaven. Furthermore God is unfair for condemning sinners who don't want to be condemned. Thus, the trend in the world today is for financial, violent, and sexual crimes to be forgiven without the need for repentance and those that wish to put an end to these sins are considered hateful. We see the results of this situation in the rapidly deteriorating state of society.

Once forgiven always forgiven?

Another popular misconception is that of blanket forgiveness: God forgives you at one time for all of your past and future sins so that, having repented once in the past, you no longer need to be concerned about sin. This idea is contrary to what Jesus tell us, that we are to forgive as often as forgiveness is sought for in repentance (Luke 17:3-4; Mat 6:14), and God will forgive us in the same way. He gives us additional forgiveness for each of our additional sins.

More than this, the Bible says that those who have been forgiven and fall back into sin are in a worse condition than if they had never been forgiven to begin with (Heb 6:4-5; Heb 10:26; 2 Pet 2:20). Jesus stated this idea to the cripple He had healed saying, "Sin no more lest a worse thing come upon thee" (John 5:14). It is illustrated by Jesus' parable of the unclean spirit that, having been cast out of a man, afterwards returns together with seven other unclean spirits more wicked than himself (Luke 11:24-26) to show how those who have had their guilt cleaned away can later end up again loaded with more guilt than before they were forgiven (Mat 12:44).

Things are worse for the person who has been forgiven and falls back into sin because, by doing so, they sear their conscience and become less susceptible to the influence of the Holy Spirit. Even if they fear the consequences of, and are sorry about, their sin, after repeating it often enough without real repentance, their consciences become so desensitised to the Holy Sprit's call that they are no long able to repent. As in the case of Esau, they can no longer obtain forgiveness (Heb 12:17) no matter how often or earnestly they ask for it, because they have sinned against the Holy Spirit. Only by experiencing a "repentance... not to be repented of" (2 Cor 7:10) as described in the chapter "True Repentance", can a relapsed sinner be re-justified before God.

Forgiveness Revoked

Additionally there are various texts in the Bible that directly state that past forgiveness can be revoked. For example, we have the parable of the unmerciful servant (Mat 18:23-34). The king mercifully forgave the servant's debt, but the forgiveness was withdrawn because he did not show mercy to his fellow servants. The biblical principle that whoever breaks one commandment is guilty of all (Jam 2:10) implies that whoever has one unforgiven sin has no sins forgiven. The Bible also makes it clear that anyone who has obtained righteousness (i.e. had all of their sins forgiven), but who afterwards "commit iniquity all his righteousnesses shall not be remembered; but for his iniquity that he hath committed, he shall die for it" (Eze 33:13 see also Eze 3:20; 18:24; 33:12-13) This is saying that all of the forgiveness of past sin they had obtained will be revoked. If God's forgiveness can be revoked it means that it is probationary, and can only be retained under certain conditions. These conditions are clearly spelt out in the scripture; we must maintain our forgiveness by continuing to exercise the same repentance and faith by which we obtained it in the first place (Col 2:6). Any lapse in our repentance results in a lapse in our forgiveness.

Some insist that past forgiveness can never be revoked because God follows the principle of forgive and forget. They turn to some texts in support:

> **Mic 7:19** thou wilt cast all their sins into the depths of the sea.
>
> **Jer 31:34** saith the LORD: for I will forgive their iniquity, and I will remember their sin no more.

Both of these texts tell us that God *will* one day forget sins that have been forgiven, not that he *has* already done this. Sins are not forgiven and forgotten at the same time. When this will take place was clearly explained by the apostle Peter at Pentecost. He said that sins which have been repented of will be blotted out when the times of refreshing come (Acts 3:19), not before. The day of atonement service in the temple shows that the record of sins forgiven throughout the year remained in the temple until the day of atonement when the temple was cleansed from its record of sin (Lev 16:16-30). Those who did not observe the day of atonement by afflicting their hearts in repentance lost whatever forgiveness they had obtained throughout the year (Lev 23:27-29). It is in the context of the yearly day of atonement service that Psalms tells us that God removed Israel's past transgressions (Ps 103:12).

Maintaining Forgiveness

Satan does not care whether you believe and hope in God or not, as long as he can keep you from repentance. He wants us to think that as long as we are sorry for the expected consequences of our sins, repentance is not necessary for forgiveness. While God's love is unconditional, His forgiveness is not. The Bible teaches that forgiveness can only be obtained through heartfelt repentance and forgiveness must be maintained by continual repentance. This applies to both God's forgiveness and man's forgiveness. God extends his love to all who have sinned against Him, so that they may come to Him in repentance. His servants are called to imitate this example. Forgiveness is not about avoiding negative feelings and making anyone feel good about themselves but about setting people free from the bondage of sin. God forgives us so that we can freely demonstrate whether or not we truly reject our sinfulness and desire holiness, unencumbered by the chains of our past sin.

On the Day of Judgment it will not matter whether our past sins were forgiven at some points, but whether we have taken advantage of His forgiveness to overcome and abandon sin altogether (Rev 3:21). God will judge if our repentance has been genuine or if it was just a ruse to escape punishment. If it has been genuine then our forgiveness is confirmed, otherwise it is revoked, because God will not be trifled with.

Godly Fear

To Fear or Not to Fear

Did you know that "The fear of the LORD *is* the beginning of wisdom" is stated 3 times in the bible? **(Ps 111:10; Prov 1:7; 9:10)**. Many believe that, because of man's imperfect understanding of God in the Old Testament, there was a need to fear Him, but since Jesus came to reveal that God is love, the need for literal fear is no longer necessary. They cite:

> **1 John 4:18** There is no fear in love; but perfect love casteth out fear.

> **2 Tim 1:7** For God hath not given us the spirit of fear; but of power, and of love, and of a sound mind.

Despite this, the New Testament, in many other places, reiterates the need to fear God **(2 Cor 7:1; Eph 5:21; Col 3:22; Heb 12:28; 1 Pet 2:17; Rev 14:7)**. How can we fear God and not fear Him at the same time? Some resolve this dilemma by claiming that the word translated as fear does not actually mean literal fear, but to respect, reverence, honour, and admire. However, the word 'fear' in the Old Testament is translated from two Hebrew words (יָרֵא yare') and (עָרַץ ` arats). The first means 'to frighten' and is translated as either 'fear', 'dread', 'afraid' or 'terrible' 99% of the time. It is only translated as 'reverence' in three of over three hundred. The other word means to 'be frightened', to be distressed by anxiety, to dread, or to be in awe (which used to mean terror). A modern dictionary definition of fear is that it is a distressing emotion or anxiety caused by anticipation of impending danger. So, are we to be anxious of impending danger at the approach of God, or just admire and reverence Him?

Imagine standing on a high cliff, would you carelessly approach the edge, or would you be afraid of falling and take the necessary precautions? If you fall, the terms on which you encounter the ground is determined by the law of gravity and the distance between you and the hard ground below. It would be much better for you to approach the ground on your own terms by carefully climbing down from your perch towards the ground. The fact is that neither the cliff not the ground below is out to hurt you, but you will die if, by your own carelessness, you do fall. You would be a fool to think otherwise.

> **Prov 14:16** A wise man feareth, and departeth from evil: but the fool [is carless] and is [over] confident.

Godly Fear

This is the same as your standing with respect to God. You stand a long way below His perfect holiness and if you do nothing to approach God by your own choice, the immutable law of heaven dictates on what terms you will encounter him in the final judgement. Since God is not willing that any should perish, He has provided a way for us to safely approach Him and warned us of the consequences of not doing so. If you choose not to follow God's instructions, the outcome is inescapable.

God's Favourites?

Many say that believers who worship or "have a relationship" with God are exempt from judgement, or more precisely that their verdict is predetermined, so they don't need to worry about it. In the cliff analogy, they aren't worried about the consequences of falling because they believe they have a parachute they call grace. They like to think they are like a student taking an exam whose grade is already decided having secured their teacher's unmerited favour through gifts and praise. Having gained this unmerited favour, other than going through the motions, the student need not make any efforts to learn or demonstrate what he has learnt. Giving out such favours in exchange for gifts or bootlicking is the very definition of corruption.

The truth is that God extends grace to everyone, even those who hate Him, and grace is not a parachute that neutralizes the judgment. Both the new and old testaments make it clear that it is the saints (who have certainly obtained grace) who need to fear God and His judgement **(Ps 119:120)**.

> **Ps 89:7** God is greatly to be feared in the assembly of the saints, and to be had in reverence of all [them that are] about him.

In this verse the word fear is (עָרַץ ʻarats) and the word reverence is (יָרֵא yare'). This text is mirrored in New Testament:

> **Heb 12:28** Wherefore we receiving a kingdom... let us have grace, whereby we may serve God acceptably with reverence and godly fear:

This time the word fear is translated from the Greek word (εὐλάβεια ev-la'-6ei-a) meaning caution and the word reverence from the Greek word (αἰδώς ai-dōs') is elsewhere translated as shamefacedness, both of which convey the idea of anxiety about danger. Why then, if God is love and, in his mercy, has given grace to his servants, does the Bible keep insisting that we need to feel anxiety instead of feeling assured and confident?

Justice for all

Jesus told many parables including: the ten virgins, the wedding feast, the unfaithful servant, the wheat and the tares etc., to explain that there will be many believers who feel assured of their salvation but will discover too late that their confidence was misplaced and had cause to fear. In the last day they will cry "Lord, Lord," to no avail. We also read that after Pentecost God slew the believing Annanias and Saphira because they did not fear Him.

> **Acts 5:11** And great fear came upon all the church, and upon as many as heard these things.

Grace is not a parachute that you can just deploy and coast carelessly to the ground. The Bible makes it clear that, unlike a student who has secured unmerited favour, a Christian seeking a favourable verdict in the judgment, must do more than just go through the motions: he needs to strive to receive a good reward, because the consequence of failure is catastrophic:

> **1Cor 9:24-27** Know ye not that they which run in a race run all, but one receiveth the prize? So run, that ye may obtain. And every man that striveth for the mastery is temperate in all things. Now they do it to obtain a corruptible crown; but we an incorruptible. I therefore so run, not as uncertainly; so fight I, not as one that beateth the air: But I keep under my body, and bring it into subjection: lest that by any means, when I have preached to others, I myself should be a castaway.

The Bible reiterates that it is not just the wicked but those who serve God need to fear Him.

> **Heb 10:31** The Lord shall judge his people. [It is] a fearful thing to fall into the hands of the living God

> **Heb 12:28-29** serve God acceptably with reverence and godly fear, for our God is a consuming fire

> **Rom 1:18** For the wrath of God is revealed from heaven against all ungodliness and unrighteousness of men, who hold the truth in unrighteousness;

> **1Pet 1:17** And if ye call on the Father, who without respect of persons judgeth according to every man's work, pass the time of your sojourning in fear:

Now some would respond that those who have obtained grace only need to fear if they are not striving to keep the commandments. They misinterpret the verse:

> **Eccl 12:13** Let us hear the conclusion of the whole matter: Fear God, and keep his

commandments: for this is the whole duty of man.

Instead, the verse says that even those who are keeping the commandments need to fear. For example:

> **Jer 9:25** Behold, the days come, saith the LORD, that I will punish all *them which are* circumcised with the uncircumcised;

It is impossible to escape the Biblical command for Christians to fear God, but if He so loved the world that He gave His only begotten son that whosoever believeth on Him has everlasting life (John 3:16), and has indeed passed from death unto life (John 5:24; 1 John 3:14) what is there to be insecure about?

Godly Fear

Those who fear heights are not terrified of the ground, but of the danger of being far away from the ground. Likewise, those who love God are not afraid of his presence, but of the danger of being far from Him, of drifting away from God: the danger of thinking we are close to Him, when we are not. Godly fear is the fear of becoming complacent or self-assured that our current understanding and acceptance of the gospel is sufficient to save us.

> **Prov 16:25** There is a way that seemeth right unto a man, but end there are the ways of death.

In the parable of the sower, Jesus taught that to those receive it, but do not properly understand it, the gospel is ineffective (Matt 13:13-14, 18-19, 23; Jer 5:20-21). Hearing they do not really understand and seeing they do not really perceive Being complacent about their understanding and presuming that their belief in God is sufficient they:

> **Rom 1:21-22** became vain in their imaginations, and their foolish heart was darkened. Professing themselves to be wise, they became fools.

They are like the five foolish virgins or the Pharisee who stood up to pray, who feel secure of their place among the saints in heaven.

> **1Thess 5:3** For when they shall say, Peace and safety; then sudden destruction cometh upon them… and they shall not escape.

So, while Christians are to come "boldly unto the throne of grace" (Heb 4:16), they are to do so in fear, recognising that their own hearts are "deceitful above all things and desperately wicked" (Jer 17:9). They should fear that they may be motivated by selfishness rather than love, that their faith may be presumption, their repentance may be like that of Balaam, Esau, and Judas (Mat 27:3), which needs to be repented of (2 Cor 7:10). This is what Paul meant when he said "Examine yourselves... prove your own selves." (2 Cor 13:5)

Fear of Missing out

David says of God "there is forgiveness with thee, that thou mayest be feared" (Ps 130:4), not fear because He might not forgive us but because we might miss obtaining it. Godly fear is not about being afraid of God's justice but fearing that we come short of His grace. It is about fearing that we might be self-deceived about our standing with God, thinking we are spiritually "rich and increased with goods and in need of nothing" while being "poor and blind and naked" (Rev 3:17), or thinking we are spiritually alive, while being spiritually dead (Rev 3:1).

This is why Jesus said, "blessed are the poor in spirit for theirs is the kingdom of heaven" (Mat 5:3). Those who think they are spiritually whole thinking themselves "to have already attained" and not needing to "press towards the mark" will miss "the prize of the high calling of God" (Phi 3:12,14). Wisdom is found in those who, fearing the deceitfulness of their own hearts, are not satisfied with their spiritual condition, and recognizing their spiritual poverty, humbly and earnestly seek more of God's grace. God says:

> Isa 66:2 to this man will I look, even to him that is poor and of a contrite spirit, and trembleth at my word.

Will you fear God enough to plead with Him to give you spiritual eyesight, or are you fine just as you are?

> Heb 4:1 Let us therefore fear, lest a promise being left [us] of entering into his rest, any of you should seem to come short of it.
>
> Phil 2:12 Wherefore, my beloved... work out your own salvation with fear and trembling.

False Christs

God is Love

The Bible emphasises that God's nature is love. (Jn 3:16) Unfortunately many people, even professed Christians, seem to have no real understanding of what that means. Majoring in minors, some like to expound on the different Greek words translated as 'love' in the Bible. The most common being *agapē* which is often translated 'charity' and refers to matters of principle and duty. The other being *phileō*, which is translated as 'brotherly love' and refers to the affections, sentiment, or feelings. However, whether God's love proceeds from His feelings towards His creatures or His duty towards them does not really help us to understand the love of God. What we want to know is: how does God's love operate and what does it do for us? What does "God is love" mean for us? To understand God's love, we need to consider what happens how it intersects with man's sin. Most obviously, it results in God being merciful and long-suffering:

> **Rom 5:8** God commendeth his love toward us, in that, while we were yet sinners, Christ died for us.
>
> **Eph 2:4** God... is rich in mercy, for his great love wherewith he loved us,

Mercy is commonly considered the counterpart to justice and so God's mercy and justice are viewed by many as a paradox of Christianity; two opposing principles that must both be satisfied. On one hand God's love is commonly portrayed as eclipsing his justice, which today is considered a dirty word and kept out of sight. Alternatively, others live in fear of God's justice with scant consideration of His love. Both perspectives arise from an incorrect (pagan) understanding of the love and justice of God. Properly understood according to the Bible, there is no paradox between God's love (or mercy) and His justice.

The reality is that love cannot exist without justice: Love without justice is nothing more than indulgent despotism, and justice without love is simply oppression. Both are evils. It is simply not possible to have any kind of balance between indulgent despotism and oppression that can be considered just or loving. Others argue that unbelievers are subject to God's justice while believers are subject to His love as if God were bipolar, each extreme being triggered by your attitude towards Him, but Jesus explained that is not so:

> **Matt 5:45** That ye may be the children of your Father which is in heaven: for he maketh his sun to rise on the evil and on the good, and sendeth rain on the just and on the unjust.

Love is in fact expressed though justice, just as much as justice is expressed through love. To relieve oppression by arresting the oppressor is an act of love. To grant a reward to a victor or overcomer is an act of justice. Those who enter heaven will do so just as much out of God's justice as out of His love, and those who go to hell will do so just as much out of God's love as out of His justice. Heaven would be intolerable to those who hate God, and going to hell would be unfair to those who by God's grace overcome sin in their life.

Baal or Jehovah

It is not possible to worship the true God if we are confused about His character, which defines His personality, or who His is. Neither a god who is unjust or unloving, nor one who is oppressive or despotically indulgent is the God of the Bible. God Himself declares:

> **Exod 34:6-7** And the LORD passed by before him, and proclaimed, The LORD, The LORD God, merciful and gracious, longsuffering, and abundant in goodness and truth, Keeping mercy for thousands, forgiving iniquity and transgression and sin, and that will by no means clear the guilty.

The problem of misconstruing God is a serious one. There are many mainstream Christians today who think they know the God of the Bible and have a personal relationship with Him but are worshipping an idol of their own imagination. Israel had this exact problem in the days of Elijah. They had been duped into worshipping Baal thinking He was the god of Israel because the name Baal just means 'The Lord'. Baal was considered the lord of heaven and earth who blessed his worshippers with material prosperity: with joy, fertility, and bountiful harvests.

In this regard he was not much different from Jehovah who also claimed to be the lord of heaven and earth and similarly promised material blessings to those who worshipped and obeyed him. While the worship of Baal was carried out to suit the cultural context of the local people and differed in style from the worship of Jehovah, the theological claims of both were strikingly similar. Despite Elijah proving at Mt. Carmel that Jehovah was a different person from Baal **(1 King 18:21-39)**, the children of Israel continued to worship Baal centuries later under his Babylonian name Tammuz, the god who died and rose again from the dead to give life to his people (Eze 8:14).

Two Characters

Given their similar claims, the only real difference between Jehovah and Baal was that of character. One could say Baal was like an indulgent father while Jehovah disciplined his children. This is clear from the Canaanite version of the Genesis account. In it the father of the gods, El, had chosen the supposedly severe and fearsome ruler of the deep, Yam, to reign over all of heaven and earth. This upset Baal, the sun god, who refused to submit to Yam's authority and defeated him to become the undisputed lord of heaven and earth and the benefactor of mankind. While both Yam and Baal blessed their worshippers and got angry with and destroyed their enemies at various times, Yam did not overlook the moral failings of his own worshippers and disciplined them. Baal, on the other hand, was considered a kind, loving God who was tolerant of his worshipper's failings and lived to save them from Yam's punishments. Yam and Baal represent the two sides of the pagan paradox; Yam was oppressive while Baal was the indulgent despot.

Since it was Jehovah who had lost control of this mankind to Lucifer at the Garden of Eden, and it was Jehovah who had brought the flood up the earth, and who destroyed the armies of Egypt in the Red Sea, we can readily identify his caricature in the figure of Yam. The long-suffering mercy of Jehovah in leading humanity to repentance, was irrelevant to those who chose not to repent. This is why the Canaanites were terrified of Jehovah as we read.

> **Gen 35:5** And they journeyed: and the terror of God was upon the cities that were round about them.

After all Jehovah did expel Adam from his Eden home and cursed the entire world for eating the wrong snack. He rejected Cain for offering the wrong sacrifice. He banned Moses from entering Canaan for striking the rock one time too many. He cursed all of Israel and thirty-six men died because Achan was selfish. He slew Uzzah because he put out his hand to steady the ark. He destroyed seven thousands of Israel because David foolishly counted the people. He slew his own prophet because he stopped to have something to eat on his way home after rebuking Jeroboam. He struck down Annanias and Saphira for keeping back a small portion of what they had promised. Jehovah will by no means clear the guilty whether they worship him or not, and so He is to be feared by all the earth (Ps 33:8, 96:9) since "God is no respecter of

Understanding Christianity

persons" (Acts 40:34)

> **Jer 9:25** saith the LORD... I will punish all *them which are* circumcised with the uncircumcised;

On the other hand, there is no fear in the worship of Baal as he never punishes those who worship him but promises to save them from punishment. Baal gives them comfort, that despite their imperfections he will save them from condemnation. He promises them peace and safety and encourages them to come before him in confident assurance. They are sure he accepts their worship and that because of it, they will reap his bountiful blessings. His worship is pleasing to them. They feel secure in his kindness and care. They imitate Baal's tolerance for each other's sins. Accordingly, His worshippers come before him without any fear: self-assured, self-confident and self-satisfied.

A father that loves his children not only rewards them but, for their own good, he also corrects them when necessary. Discipline is nevertheless unpleasant for both parents and children. An indulgent father does not discipline because he cares more about his own pleasure than for the future well-being of his children. Jesus himself declares

> **Rev 3:19** As many as I love, I rebuke and chasten: be zealous therefore, and repent.

As the Bible says, "happy *is* the man whom God correcteth." (Job 5:17-18; Pro 3:11-12)

> **Heb 12:5-8**, My son, despise not thou the chastening of the Lord... For whom the Lord loveth he chasteneth, and scourgeth every son whom he receiveth. If ye endure chastening, God dealeth with you as with sons; for what son is he whom the father chasteneth not? But if ye be without chastisement, whereof all are partakers, then are ye bastards, and not sons.

The First Lie

The first lie of the serpent to Eve was that God would not punish her disobedience (Gen 3:4). He is still repeating this lie to Christians today. He wants us to focus on God's love, kindness, and mercy, but overlook his justice and hatred of sin. He wants us to read the first part of John 8:11 "Jesus said unto her, neither do I condemn thee", but skip over what immediately followed "go, and sin no more." He wants us to worship Baal instead of Jehovah.

While Satan is busy getting us to worship an idol god that tolerates our sins

False Christs

and will not punish our wrongdoing. Jesus warns us in Matthew 7:21-23 that He will not tolerate iniquity in those who worship Him, no matter what good works they perform in his name. As the apostle Paul said

> **Heb 10:26-27** For if we sin willfully after that we have received the knowledge of the truth, there remaineth no more sacrifice for sins, But a certain fearful looking for of judgment and fiery indignation, ...

> **Heb 10:30-31** For we know him that hath said, Vengeance *belongeth* unto me, I will recompense, saith the Lord... The Lord shall judge his people. It is a fearful thing to fall into the hands of the living God.

As we saw before, there can be no love or mercy without justice. It is because God is love that He will punish wrongdoing. First in this life, hoping to bring those who do evil to repentance so to be able to save them, and failing that, in the second resurrection to eradicate evil for the good of the rest of his creatures. It is also because of love that God extends his grace, delaying the last day as long as possible "not willing that any should perish, but that all should come to repentance" **(2Pet 3:9)**

Do not misconstrue the grace or long-suffering mercy of God so as to divorce His love from His justice and thereby continue doing evil **(Ecc 8:11)**. God is either who He says He is, the righteous king of heaven and earth, or an indulgent despotic pretender like Baal. The scripture commands us to "Fear God and give glory to him; for the hour of his judgement is come" **(Rev 14:7)**, which God do you serve?

> **Josh 24:14-15** Now therefore fear the LORD, and serve him in sincerity and in truth: and put away the gods which your fathers served on the other side of the flood [Baal], and in Egypt; and serve ye the LORD. And if it seem evil unto you to serve the LORD, choose you this day whom ye will serve; whether the gods which your fathers served... but as for me and my house, we will serve the LORD.

www.ingramcontent.com/pod-product-compliance
Lightning Source LLC
Chambersburg PA
CBHW072210070526
44585CB00015B/1275